THE POTTED GARDEN

THE POTTED GARDEN

CREATING GREAT CONTAINER GARDENS

BECKIE FOX

Photographs by Roger Yip

A Pearson Company
Toronto

Canadian Cataloguing in Publication Data

Fox, Beckie
    The potted garden : creating great container gardens

Includes index.
ISBN 0-13-091573-4

1. Container gardening. I. Title.

SB418.F68   2002   635.9'86   C2001-903604-3

ISBN 0-13-091573-4

Editorial Director, Trade Division: Andrea Crozier
Acquisitions Editor: Andrea Crozier
Managing Editor: Tracy Bordian
Copy Editor: Nancy Carroll
Proofreader: Nick Gamble
Art Direction: Mary Opper
Cover Design: Mary Opper
Interior Design: Sarah Battersby
Cover Image: Roger Yip
Author Photograph: Bert Klassen
Production Manager: Kathrine Pummell
Page Layout: Janet Zanette

1 2 3 4 5   KR   06 05 04 03 02

Printed and bound in Canada.

ATTENTION: CORPORATIONS
Books are available at quantity discounts with bulk purchase for educational, business, or sales promotional use. For information, please email or write to: Pearson PTR Canada, Special Sales, PTR Division, 26 Prince Andrew Place, Don Mills, Ontario, M3C 2T8. Email ss.corp@pearsoned.com. Please supply: title of book, ISBN, quantity, how the book will be used, date needed.

Visit the Pearson PTR Canada Web site! Send us your comments, browse our catalogues, and more. **www.pearsonptr.ca**

Prentice
Hall
Canada

A Pearson Company

For Michael,
with love and gratitude

contents

acknowledgments

Writing a book is largely a labor of love—and sometimes just plain labor. Several people generously provided expertise, suggestions and support, all of which were tremendously helpful. It's my pleasure to acknowledge their contributions here.

Thanks go to Andrea Crozier and Tracy Bordian of Prentice Hall Canada for guiding *The Potted Garden* from an idea to what you hold in your hand. I'm also grateful to Nancy Carroll for her careful copy editing.

Photographer Roger Yip, whose creative eye and technical expertise help tell the story visually, was also a good sport during a long, hot summer. Many thanks also to the gardeners who graciously allowed their gardens to be photographed.

Good friends provided helpful advice and expertise, too. Heather White offered valuable feedback on the manuscript, and Judith Adam was generous with her gardening knowledge and encouragement.

My warmest thanks are reserved for my family—husband Michael, son Matthew and daughter Katherine—who were unwavering with their support, patience and enthusiasm for this project.

I've come to realize that it's the people in our lives who influence us to become gardeners, not the plants. In my case, it was my father, Gerald Hanes, who always made time and space for roses, tomatoes and whatever else he could fit in. His example—both in and out of the garden—spoke volumes, and this book is also lovingly dedicated to his memory. Cutting tall pink zinnias in a large plot beside our house for the kitchen table is my earliest memory of a garden—and the one I treasure most.

Beckie Fox
Unionville, Ontario

foreword

I started growing plants in containers for the same reason many people do: I was new to gardening and containers seemed a lot easier than tackling an entire garden where there were too many holes to dig, too many decisions to make and way too much space to contemplate. A few pots, a few plants and a couple of bags of soil—what could be simpler? My first attempts were fun—and probably laid the foundation for a love of gardening—but when I look back on those forlorn petunias struggling in compacted soil with not enough water and no food, it's no wonder my results were disappointing.

A couple of decades have passed since my foray into container gardening. Today, I grow far too many plants in way too many containers—mainly because I love the chance to experiment with new color combinations, try new plants, create outlandish surprises. Every year is different, and equally exciting. I'd be less than candid if I didn't own up to some real duds, but these never seem to spoil my enthusiasm. For me, a garden without a few pots, baskets and planters would be a dismal sight indeed.

It's my hope that the ideas and information in this book help you create a container garden that suits your style, your budget and your space. Most of all, I hope you discover that it's a fun and exciting way to personalize your garden.

getting started

1

*"There are no gardening mistakes,
only experiments."*

~Janet Kilburn Phillips

Gardeners nurture plants for many reasons—gone are the days when we gardened primarily to put food on our table and fend off hunger. You may relish the scientific challenge of growing the tallest sunflower or the earliest tomato. Perhaps you are more interested in designing a floral extravaganza to admire from your window. Or maybe you simply take up a trowel as a way to step out of an increasingly chaotic lifestyle and into a calming zone where a few basics—sun, water, soil and plants—afford you a chance to reflect, meditate and decompress. Return those five phone calls or deadhead the geraniums? It's an easy choice for gardeners. Besides, geraniums don't talk back.

Just as the reasons for gardening vary from person to person, so do levels of commitment. You may spend almost every day puttering, potting and planting until the sun sets, savoring the process as much as the plants. Your neighbor, on the other hand, may prefer a more low-maintenance approach.

The reasons for gardening in containers are as varied as those for gardening in general. When you run short of space in your traditional garden, you may turn to containers as a way to grow more plants, or tuck in a container or two of colorful annuals in areas where perennials have finished blooming. Containers also let you test-drive specimens you've not grown before or control an invasive favorite. If you garden on the concrete floor of a balcony or roof, it's the only option. However, the most significant reason for container gardening's popularity is the amazing creativity it affords. The pairing of a gorgeous terra-cotta pot with contrasting leaf shapes and complementary flower colors placed at the bend of a path can make a visitor stop and admire its beauty. (You may claim to enjoy the solitude of gardening, but you'll love it when visitors recognize your efforts.) Similarly, a cluster of pots with plants can help blend a patio or deck with the garden beyond and create an inviting setting in which to relax or entertain guests.

All gardening is an exciting blend of art and science: our knowledge of how plants grow keeps them beautiful and healthy, and our creativity to display them in imaginative ways enhances our surroundings. This balance is especially crucial when growing plants in containers to create decorative accents—even the most elegant terra-cotta pot looks woebegone if the plants in it are struggling to keep their flowery heads aloft. Conversely, the healthiest plants may be less than riveting if we don't take time to match them with suitable containers displayed in appealing ways.

The first—and arguably most important—principle to understand is that growing plants in pots is different from growing plants in a traditional garden. The soil is different, the watering and fertilizing needs are different, and the plants are chosen with different criteria—they grow differently in a container, and they require different planting methods. There's nothing complicated about these differences, but understanding them determines whether you'll have a satisfying or a frustrating experience with container growing.

Plan First, Plant Later

Good container gardens usually begin with some forethought. Before putting plant to pot, ask yourself: 1. Where is the pot going to go? 2. How much time am I willing to spend caring for it? These questions are pretty basic, but you'd be surprised how many times enthusiastic gardeners (myself included) have dashed out to buy plants and pots, and planted everything in a rush, only to realize midway through the season that things are not going well. The effect isn't what we expected, or the plants are suffering, or we're tied to a watering can or…. The problem isn't a lack of gardening skills or that there's some mythical secret to achieving stunning floral displays in a pot—it's just that we didn't think things through.

But if planning is anathema to you and spontaneity is your gardening mantra, forge ahead. Gather plants that please you, an eclectic collection of pots, and plant away to your heart's content. There's no denying the gardening high you'll get when your spontaneous efforts are extremely successful. While less likely to be effective, they certainly can be. Unfortunately, whenever I've tried this, I end up standing in the driveway with a jungle of oddly matched plants, an even odder assortment of pots and no idea of where to begin. Before I know it, the sun is setting, and I still haven't planted a thing.

Assess Your Site and Your Needs

When it comes to containers, I have the same advice as real estate agents: location, location, location. Walk around your house and garden and imagine where pots might look best.

Front Entrance
Visitors to your home appreciate a warm welcome, and the front door or porch is the perfect place to add a personal statement. Just make sure your "statement" doesn't make walking to and from the front door a hazard. A hanging basket might suit here if stairs are narrow. This is a public and highly visible area, so choose plants with long-term interest, and plant containers so they are visually appealing from day one. Think about how the entranceway looks from the sidewalk or road: a few small pots filled with dainty blooms, such as lobelia (*L. erinus*) or sweet alyssum (*Lobularia maritima*) won't be noticed. Be bold. Imagine the drama of dahlias, cannas and bidens framing your entranceway.

Back Patios, Terraces and Decks

This is usually a more intimate area—often where you dine, barbecue or sit outside. Fragrant plants are appreciated here, and if the kitchen is nearby, it's the perfect spot for herbs and vegetables. On wooden decks, where standing water might create stains or cause the wood to rot, raise large planters a few inches (about 7 cm) off the surface or use plant saucers under small pots.

Steps, Walls and Fences

These areas are often boring and monotonous. A wall basket enhances a bare wall, much like a painting breaks up an interior wall. Pots planted with the same plants, one pot on each step, provide a linear, organized look. The side entrance to my house is midway along a narrow walkway bordered by a high wooden fence. I have three small half-pots along the top of the fence filled with trailing English ivy (*Hedera helix*) and Swan River daisies (*Brachyscome iberdifolia*) to soften the harshness of the fence and draw the eye to the border of plants at its base.

Windows

Not all house styles and windows suit window boxes, but if you have a traditional style house and window ledges, window boxes are a beautiful accent. One of the advantages is that the blooms are visible to the home's occupants as well as passersby. If your house doesn't have window ledges, mount boxes to the side of the house, directly below the bottom of the window. Of course, you can use shapes other than boxes. A row of matching terra-cotta pots lined up along the ledge outside a kitchen window, each planted with one perfect pansy—or whatever captures your fancy—is quite charming.

 ## Size Things Up

Large containers dominate their immediate surroundings, so site them where you want to accent your garden's good points: an entranceway, the foot of an arbor, the edge of a pond, the seating area on a deck. Don't expect a large container to camouflage an eyesore—unless the container is so large it obscures the object entirely. Hanging moss baskets from the eaves of a dilapidated metal shed or placing pots of annuals on either side of a garage door only draw attention to these structures. Instead, place a planter in another part of the yard to create a visual treat to distract viewers from your garden's less desirable features.

Small containers can be delightful, too, and are well suited to showing off the attributes of diminutive treasures like violets, stone crops (*Sedum* species or cultivars) and English daisies (*Bellis perennis*). In hurly-burly perennial and shrub borders, these charmers can be easily overwhelmed. Place a small wicker basket brimming with miniature roses near a chaise longue where each flower can be admired, or elevate a shallow bowl of hens and chicks (*Sempervivum tectorum*) on a pedestal set in a drift of creeping thyme.

Make a Focal Point

A focal point in the garden is like punctuation in a sentence: it acts as a guide for our eyes, drawing them through a space and showing them where to linger. If you have a perennial border that has a gap in midsummer, a large pot of complementary colored flowers, raised slightly above the perennial foliage, draws the eye through the bed and beyond. Or use a boldly planted urn at the intersection of paths in an ornamental vegetable garden. If you have a long path that ends at a bench, flank either end of the seat with containers to highlight the area and give it even more prominence.

Solve a Problem

If you have horrible soil that requires a few seasons of amending before you can plant, or you're in rented quarters, growing plants in containers lets you partake in all the joys of gardening regardless of your soil—or lack of it. Urban gardeners who have a tiny postage stamp–size garden where only a small area receives sunlight each day can pot up half a dozen containers and rotate them to make best use of the bit of sun they do have. Gardeners who live in a high-rise can use a long narrow balcony as a place to grow climbing morning glories, cherry tomatoes and cheerful, sturdy marigolds, rather than as a storage area for mountain bikes and other gear. For people who find bending down to their garden at ground level increasingly difficult, a series of raised planting boxes can mean the difference between abandoning gardening or being able to carry on with what they love.

Mix Equal Parts Optimism and Realism

After walking through your garden and imagining the possibilities, you've likely drawn up a list of 5, 10, 15 ideal locations. I'm probably the least credible person to tell you to be realistic—there are about three dozen containers in my small suburban garden—but it is important to understand that although there is nothing inherently difficult about growing plants in pots, container gardening does require ongoing maintenance, sometimes watering on a daily basis, for example, when days are hot and pots are small. You'll need to empty and store pots at the end of the season and replant next year. If you're already pressed for time, consider adding just two or three large containers filled with easy-to-care-for plants, and place them where you'll receive the most enjoyment from them. Remember, gardening should be fun, not a chore, and the quickest way to make gardening seem like work is to try to do too much.

Once you've decided where pots, baskets and window boxes will be placed and how involved you want to be with their care, you need to decide what container sizes and types are most appropriate, and then choose a collection of plants—climbing, cascading, upright—that complement each other, the pot and location. Container and plant choices are based on not just what's practical, but what's pleasing, too. Choose what you like, without worrying whether it's fashionable or popular. Let's consider container styles and materials first.

choosing
containers

"A pot should be
as a picture frame is for a work of art."

~Guy Wolff

Do you want a dramatic statement at your front entrance? Will you use containers to grow plants you don't have room for in your jam-packed beds and borders? Or do you live in an apartment or condominium and the only way to flex your green thumb is with big planters on a balcony? Your needs and expectations will affect the containers you choose. Once you've decided where to place your pots, planters, baskets or window boxes, it's time to choose the containers: they should be the right sizes and styles for your garden, and made of practical materials.

When I started gardening 25 years ago, I wanted to embellish a new, bare deck. I drove to the lumberyard and bought three plain eight-inch (20-cm) terra-cotta pots, planted a red geranium and two white petunias in each, and set them on the steps. At the time, there wasn't a lot of choice in containers (or container plants, for that matter). Small or even smaller? Wood or clay? That was about it. But the price was right: I still have one of the pots, and the grease pencil scrawl on the bottom says $2.39.

Today, the range of container styles, sizes and materials is mind-boggling, and the quest for the perfect pot can be a bewildering journey. Advances in manufacturing processes and the development of new plastics, resins, molds and finishes mean it's possible to find realistic and lightweight look-alikes of antique lead and stone, and many of the new pots are lighter and more frost tolerant than their predecessors. The price range is broader, too. You can still find a pot for $2.39, but it's just as likely you'll find one that costs $239. Obviously, containers in this price range are a long-term investment, since the container will be with you far longer than the plants you fill it with. Be practical. Does it offer good drainage? Is it the appropriate size?

Drainage

It's imperative that excess water be able to drain away from plant roots. There must be a hole or holes in the bottom of any container in which you intend to grow plants. Don't assume careful watering on your part will compensate for the lack of an opening to allow excess water to drain away. You'll either water too shallowly, and the plants will fail to thrive, or you'll miscalculate (usually more than once) and the roots will end up rotting in the soggy soil at the bottom where excess water pools. When the pot of your dreams has no drainage hole, place a slightly smaller plastic or fiber container (sometimes called a liner) inside. The bottom of the liner needs to sit at least an inch (2.5 cm) above the bottom of the decorative container so excess water has a place to drain.

Size

Big plants need big containers. Big containers—even those that house several plants—require less frequent watering, hold more soil, which provides more insulation for roots during extremes of heat and cold, and have more visual impact than small containers. However, small containers sometimes serve a purpose. You may want to display a collection of herbs on an antique plant stand, for example, with each plant potted individually. Just be prepared to provide more frequent attention to these small-scale displays.

Do I like it? Can I afford it? Will it last?

Once you've met the practical criteria, you can consider other factors: your style, budget and climate. If you live in Canada or in the northern states where winters remain below freezing, and you plan to leave your containers outdoors—planted or unplanted—you'll need frost-resistant containers. If, at the end of each season, you empty your plants onto the compost pile and stack the pots in the garage until next spring, lightweight, stackable pots will be a bigger priority for you than tolerance to frost. If you garden on a balcony or rooftop, and have lugged bags of potting soil up the stairs, you know soil is heavy: using lightweight plastic or wood will reduce the overall load. Even if you're not gardening several stories up, to make gardening easier, you'll want to consider the portability and weight of the containers you buy.

Finally, give some thought to the style or design of the container you're considering. Take your cue from your house, other structures in your garden and the garden's overall design. If you have a quaint Cape Cod, willow baskets and painted wood are likely a better match than formal cast-iron urns. If your garden features a restrained palate of ornamental grasses, long vistas and carefully pruned hedges, sleek concrete planters will reinforce your minimalist look. To help you decide which materials suit your style, budget and climate, consider the different container materials described on the following pages.

Terra Cotta

The sizes, ornamentation, shapes and styles offered in terra cotta are almost limitless, and the warm, natural color of the clay complements all plants and most design schemes, from blowsy, romantic cottage gardens to minimalist terraces with contemporary lines. There's no doubt the relationship between terra cotta and plants is a long-standing one—much of it is based on tradition, but there are practical reasons too.

Plants and terra cotta have been linked together for centuries (see "The Tale of Terra Cotta," page 12). The Italian phrase means "cooked earth"—more precisely, clay that's baked in a kiln. The type of clay and the temperature at which it's fired determine the durability of the finished product. Pots fired at a high heat are more frost-resistant than those fired at a lower heat because the high firing makes a harder, less porous pot. Moisture is less likely to permeate the walls, freeze and expand, causing cracks in the pot. Sometimes even soil left in a frost-resistant pot over winter can freeze, expand and put enough pressure on the sides to cause it to crack.

Terra cotta's porosity is both an advantage and disadvantage. Roots appreciate the cooling effects from the air exchange terra cotta provides, and fertilizer salts rarely build up inside pots because they're able to leach out during watering. (Most people consider the white, powdery residue on the outside a decorative characteristic of aging, but if you want to remove it, scrub with a weak solution of warm water and bleach.) Should you accidentally overwater a plant, clay absorbs excess water although it does have its limits. However, this breathability means water evaporates more quickly in a terra-cotta pot than one made from plastic or metal. Small pots that dry out too quickly can first be lined with a clear plastic bag, then filled with soil and planted. Either cut a few drainage holes in the bottom of the bag before inserting it in the pot, or punch a hole in the plastic, directly above the drainage hole, by poking a pencil or skewer up through the hole after the pot is filled with soil.

Prices of terra-cotta containers vary considerably, and as is often the case, a quality piece costs more. Generally terra cotta is less expensive than metal or reconstituted stone. Most of what's available in North America is imported from Italy or Mexico, and prices reflect the quality of workmanship, currency exchange and shipping costs. Some Mexican pots with thick walls may have been dried in the sun, rather than a kiln, and deteriorate after only a few seasons or even more quickly if exposed to a lot of water.

Terra-cotta pots can be hand-thrown or mass-produced (the clay is pressed into molds), and the latter is usually less expensive. Hand-thrown pots are more durable because the clay is "worked" into a pot shape and not forced into a mold; walls are usually thicker, too. There's no doubt a hand-thrown pot is beautiful to behold, a work of art for your garden. All terra cotta is breakable, no matter how well made, which is something to consider if you're storing a hand-crafted piece of art next to your car door over the winter.

Look for terra cotta that's labeled frost-resistant. This doesn't mean frost-proof, but will mean you're purchasing a more durable pot. According to some, the only terra cotta that reliably survives North American winters comes from Impruneta, Italy. The pale, local clay is high in iron and calcium, which means it can be fired at a higher temperature than other clays. It's extremely expensive—$50US ($75CDN) will buy a hand-thrown eight- by six-inch (20- by 15-cm) pot with a decorative band of raised fruit around the top edge. But it will probably be around for your grandchildren to inherit.

Other indications of quality to look for are more than one drainage hole in large containers and a ridge around the base to raise the bottom of the pot slightly off the surface it sits on. This will facilitate drainage.

Some terra cotta is glazed on the outside, which slows down evaporation. Eventually these finishes wear or flake off, but the pot is still serviceable, although it may have lost some of its esthetic appeal.

Maintenance

- Soak brand-new containers in water for an hour or two before planting. This prevents the unseasoned clay from wicking water away from the moist soil and leaving your plants thirsty. Rubbing a thin film of vegetable oil onto the outside surface after soaking helps slow down initial moisture loss, too.
- Terra cotta is more difficult to clean and sterilize than plastic, fiberglass and metal containers. In the fall, empty the pots and use a wire brush to loosen soil. Wash the inside with a weak bleach and water solution (one part bleach to nine parts water), rinse and store upside down under shelter.

Hastening the Aging Process

One of terra cotta's attractions is that it ages gracefully. The lichens and moss that cover old pots add a sense of permanence and character to a garden setting. (The aging process is faster with hand-thrown pots than with mass-produced versions.)

However, the process does take a few seasons. To encourage algae to grow more quickly on a new terra-cotta container, paint a thin coat of plain yogurt or buttermilk on the outside. Mixing in some soil or compost helps things along. Place the treated pot in the shade and spray occasionally with water or water mixed with liquid fertilizer. An easier method is to occasionally rub the surface of a new pot with a handful of damp garden detritus, such as grass clippings, moist soil, leaf prunings and the like.

These techniques work well with concrete containers, too. If you simply want to lighten and soften the bright orange of new terra cotta, brush on a wash of water mixed with powdered horticultural lime.

The Tale of Terra Cotta

The first terra-cotta containers were used to hold water and food—not plants—by the ancient Greeks and Romans. Eventually the material showed up in floors, fountains, sculpture and, finally, containers for growing citrus trees and decorative plants.

Small potteries dotted the countryside in England throughout the 1800s, where skills were passed down from generation to generation. The demand for different shapes and sizes increased to meet the needs of a burgeoning nursery business and an avid population of gardeners, and good potteries were adept at turning out hundreds of pots a day. The myriad sizes had different names: "a tall Tom," sometimes called "a long Tom," referred to tall, narrow pots used for plants with deep roots; "seed pans" were short and squat, perfect for germinating seeds; "thumbs and thimbles" were tiny pots used for transplants.

The most familiar shape today is a slightly flared, straight-sided pot with a wide, flat rim, called a "chime rim," which came into existence when manufacturers began mass producing terra-cotta pots using molds. (Up until the mid-1800s, when the turning mold machine was invented, all pots were hand thrown, often with rolled rims to help them retain their shape during firing.) Chime rims made it easy to stack pots, therefore saving space in the kiln when firing. Over the years, manufacturers also began making pots with thinner walls to save money on clay, which means the mass-produced pots made today are more fragile than those from the 19th century.

Hand-thrown pots are still made today by craftsman in England, Italy and North America who take pride in their own designs and turn out small quantities for loyal customers. Their pots' organic shapes and soft, rolled rims have many admirers.

Earthenware

Earthenware, another type of fired clay, shares many of terra cotta's characteristics, but is coarser and more porous. Most of the examples on the market today are imported from China or other Asian countries and feature a shiny, colored glaze on the outside, sometimes with an Oriental motif. Inside, the pots are usually an ivory shade. Often they come with a matching saucer. Those without drainage holes make beautiful containers for water gardens. Glazed earthenware pots retain moisture better than terra cotta; however, they are just as breakable and more likely to be damaged by frost than most terra-cotta pots.

Wood

Like terra cotta, wood fits into most planting schemes, from grand, formal Versailles boxes painted a crisp white to contrast with clipped spheres of boxwood, to rustic half-barrels overflowing with nasturtiums and cozy window boxes of trailing geraniums neatly underlining every window on a cottage. It's likely the second-most prevalent material used for container plantings, after terra cotta, and probably the first choice of balcony and rooftop gardeners. Balcony gardens often require large, deep containers for permanent plantings, in custom sizes, and wood is the perfect choice: it's lighter and less expensive than terra cotta, stone or metal, and it offers better insulation.

Not all wood stands up to prolonged exposure to moisture. Hardwoods such as oak and teak are rot- and moisture-resistant, but expensive. More reasonably priced softwoods like cedar, cypress and redwood resist decay and wood-destroying fungi and insects as well. More economical wood—pine and spruce, for example—are fine, too, but you'll need to treat them with a preservative, such as a sealer or a primer and paint. Make sure whatever preservative you use doesn't contain creosote or pentachlorophenol (sometimes called "penta"). Creosote is a distillate of coal tar; penta is a complex chemical compound. Both give off vapors that may injure some plants. Pressure-treated CCA wood (chromated copper arsenate), commonly used for fences and decks, is generally acceptable, although gardeners who prefer not to use any type of preservative near plants, especially food plants, use redwood or cedar containers, which can be left untreated.

If you're at all handy, wood is an easy material to work with, and you can create custom-made containers that fit your windowsills perfectly, and paint them to match your house. Use galvanized wood screws, which won't rust; and screws, not nails. Nails can easily pop out with the stress of heavy soil. It's easy to drill drainage holes in the bottom of wooden boxes or planters, or if you're making your own, leave a narrow gap between the boards at the bottom.

Maintenance

- If your wood containers are painted, you'll need to repaint every two or three years. You may want to seal them with a non-toxic preservative instead, especially if the boxes are permanently mounted on house siding.
- To prolong the life of any wooden container, line the inside with plastic before planting. Perforate the bottom of the plastic to allow for drainage. You can also buy ready-made rigid plastic or metal liners that fit standard-size wooden window boxes. Moisture will still reach the wood when excess water drains from a liner, but damp soil and fungi won't be in constant contact with the wood. Rigid liners also make planting wall-mounted window boxes simpler—plant the liner and then drop it in the already mounted window box.

Metals

The elegant lead, iron and bronze urns we see in photos of grand estates of yesteryear have a high appeal rating—and an equally high price tag. At least their not-insubstantial weight discourages theft. The highly festooned antiques are decidedly formal, and some are so ornate and detailed, they're best left unplanted, and placed on a plinth to be admired.

There are other metal containers, ones of this century, which are more attainable. Cast-iron urns with black, brown or white finishes are readily available at most garden centers—even some hardware and grocery chains. New cast-iron planters can still put a dent in a garden budget. A traditionally designed urn about 30 inches (76 cm) tall usually costs between $66 and $200US ($100 and $300CDN). Metal containers can weigh up to a few hundred pounds (about 150 kg), they retain moisture and are impervious to frost damage. Most rust over time; an undesirable characteristic for some, a bonus for gardeners seeking an instant aged look.

If new or antique cast iron, bronze and lead suit neither your taste nor your budget, you might find the simplicity of galvanized pails, boxes and tubs more appealing. Three galvanized pails nailed near the top of a wooden fence and filled with blue and white trailing lobelia (*Lobelia erinus*) are charming and whimsical in a casual setting. You can easily drill holes in the bottom, if necessary. The shininess of new galvanized steel dulls over time—but it won't rust.

Heavy gauge steel wire—intricate filigree confections or more basic frames of connected concentric circles—are often used for moss-lined round, hanging baskets or rectangular baskets for walls or window ledges, sometimes called "hayracks" or "mangers." Look for sturdy construction with hanging chains (or hooks, in the case of wall baskets) that will support the weight of wet soil and plants. Openings between the wires should be spaced closely enough to keep the moss in place.

Maintenance

Admittedly, cast iron rusts over time, but it usually makes the urn look like a family antique, rather than a recent acquisition. If rust holds little appeal for you, occasionally remove the rust and paint with a rust-proof enamel. A knowledgeable paint expert at a full-service hardware store should be able to advise you.

 ## Stone and Concrete

Probably the most durable—and most expensive—container material is composition, or reconstituted, stone. (Forget about real stone such as marble or sandstone—its rarity makes it forbiddingly dear.) Composition stone, a mix of concrete and crushed stone first made in the 18th century, looks much like real stone. It can be cast into various shapes, and acquires an attractive patina of moss and lichens as it ages. Composition stone and the less costly cast concrete containers provide good insulation during fluctuating temperatures, and they retain moisture. Durable and classic, a reconstituted stone container is the epitome of classic elegance. Cast concrete planters are sometimes more utilitarian- and contemporary-looking than stone. Those made with an exposed-aggregate surface have a rugged simplicity that complements an urban, industrial look. Placement requires forethought—it takes more than one person to move a large concrete container. Reconstituted stone and concrete pots are frost-resistant, while large, well made examples are virtually frost-proof.

Maintenance

Use water and a soft brush to clean reconstituted stone; a stiff brush is fine for cast concrete.

Plastic

Once frequently rejected solely on esthetic grounds, plastic containers have had a tremendous makeover in recent years. New designs, manufacturing processes and finishes mean many of them easily fool even the most discerning members of the style police. Plastic has several advantages over other materials. High on the list of desirable characteristics is its affordability, although the best-looking terra cotta look-alikes are often the same price as the real thing. But if you need to outfit a bare balcony or deck quickly, or plan to grow all of your vegetables in large containers, economically priced plastic pots may be your salvation.

Soil stays moist two or three times longer in a plastic pot than it does in one made from terra cotta or wood. However, its ability to retain moisture does have a downside; fertilizer salts can't leach out of the sides of the pot, and may reach levels high enough to burn plant roots. Don't overfeed—or overwater—plants growing in plastic containers. Some models come with reservoirs to hold water and a capillary or wick system draws water as needed. These are good options for people whose lifestyle warrants a low-maintenance setup.

Plastic offers little insulation—roots in a dark-colored hanging plastic basket may cook on a hot, sunny day. Lower-quality plastic containers will fade in the sun and become brittle when exposed to winter's extreme temperatures. Good plastic is labeled UV stabilized.

The Story of Coade Stone

One of the most famous formulas for reconstituted stone had its beginnings in 1769, when George and Eleanor Coade bought a factory in England that made terra-cotta-type artificial stone. When George died, Eleanor and her daughter continued experimenting. Eventually, they came up with a weatherproof material, less easily eroded than natural stone, and the factory became known for its beautifully designed, classically styled containers and figures. Unfortunately, when the factory closed in 1840, about 20 years after the daughter died, the formula for the mixture was lost. Several manufacturers attempted to mimic what Eleanor and her daughter concocted, but never recreated the mixture exactly. The containers of Coade stone that still remain are highly coveted.

Today's manufacturers of quality reconstituted stone are mainly found in England: Haddonstone and Chilstone are two well-known companies.

Be Creative

With a brush and acrylic paint, you can turn a plain plastic flower pot into a lead or cast-iron look-alike. Plastic is suitable for a wide range of paint techniques. Use your imagination, and don't be afraid to do something different. A collection of inexpensive, plain plastic containers painted with colorful swirls, stripes or polka dots goes well with retro '70s-style décor—if you're so disposed. Sometimes good taste and subtlety are overrated.

- If you're mimicking a natural material such as stone or iron, pick a realistic-shaped pot, and be sure to cover all exposed surfaces, including the top two inches (5 cm) on the inside of the pot.

- Creating a new look for a plastic pot is often a multi-step process involving two or more paint colors; every once in a while, take a step back and survey your work. It's easier to add a dab or two more than it is to remove them. And if you position your "fakes" somewhere in the garden where they can't be scrutinized close up, you'll fool more people. Finish painted pots with two coats of polyurethane varnish.

- For a lead look, use a base coat of silver paint, cover with black paint diluted with water (a drop of liquid dishwashing detergent helps the black wash adhere to the base coat). Lightly dab on random patches of black. Let dry and dab on more as needed. Then take flat blue paint and very lightly and sparingly dab a bit on raised areas to create highlights. Blend the edges.

- For a rusted iron finish, look for rust paint kits in craft stores and follow the directions. Make sure you do this procedure outdoors and wear protective gloves and eye protection; the materials are very corrosive.

- For a stone or concrete finish, mix some sand into paint and brush it onto the surface. Or mix equal parts of glue and water; spread a thin coat over the plastic; then add sand to the mixture and apply over top as your finish coat.

 ## Fiberglass

Easy for manufacturers to mold and paint, fiberglass containers come in a variety of shapes and sizes, especially large sizes that would be extremely costly and heavy if made from the natural materials they often mimic—lead, stone, ceramic or wood. I've been completely fooled by black "cast-iron" urns—until I realize I can pick them up, one in each hand, because they're fiberglass.

Fiberglass is less expensive than stone, but more costly than plastic, terra cotta and wood. It offers little in the way of insulation, but can be left outdoors over winter and retains moisture well.

 ## Fiber

Not everyone considers the pebbly cardboard-type containers, in which many plants come home from the nursery, a long-term option, but the material makes an economical, unobtrusive receptacle. The material has an earthy look—the dark brown color resembles soil—and a container fades into the background, letting its contents take center stage. Admittedly, a fiber container may not be the look you're after for a formal entrance, but it's practical for hanging baskets and window boxes filled with trailing plants that soon disguise most of the container. I'd take a hanging fiber pot over a white plastic hanging basket any day. Lasting only a couple of seasons, fiber is lightweight, biodegradable and more porous than terra cotta. The pressed fibers are usually recycled paper, sometimes wood fiber.

The Kitchen Sink and Everything Else

Frankly, the list of container materials could go on and on. As long as the two tenets mentioned at the beginning—it holds soil and allows drainage—are followed, you can widen your search to, well, anything: found objects like old wheelbarrows, running shoes, olive oil tins, birdbaths, wooden fruit crates, bushel baskets, wicker baskets, decayed logs, discarded kettles, enamel colanders, a child's wagon—the list goes on. Any of these may be more suitable and satisfying than a store-bought *objet d'art*. After all, good gardens benefit from a healthy dose of imagination.

Now that you've chosen containers to suit your style, budget and climate, you may think the next step is acquiring the plants, but that would be jumping ahead. There are a few more practical matters to consider before heading out on a plant-buying spree. For instance, you'll need to have the right kind of soil on hand to turn those empty pots into the kinds of places your plants will want to come home to.

Pot Feet and Saucers

Two accessories container gardeners often find useful are pot feet and pot saucers. Pot feet come in threes and raise a large pot a few inches (about 7 cm) above the surface it sits on. Raising a pot off the ground allows water to drain more freely out the bottom drainage holes and air to circulate across the bottom. The pot feet are spaced equidistantly around the base to keep the container stable. Terra cotta or cast iron sets sold at garden centers can be highly decorative—frogs, duck feet or elegant acanthus leaves, for example—with prices ranging from a few dollars to nearly $50 (U.S. $80). Simple objects at hand are economical alternatives. Small blocks of wood, bricks or three small pot saucers turned upside down are perfectly serviceable. The key is to use objects of uniform size with flat tops.

Pot saucers can be used with any size container and are most commonly paired with terra cotta, earthenware and plastic pots. They're beneficial if you're concerned about water damage to the sisal carpet on the balcony or the wood surface of a deck, for instance. Glazed terra cotta or plastic saucers are the most watertight. Saucers need to be large enough to hold overflows. Remove any water that remains in the saucer an hour after watering. Also check saucers after a rain.

the right soil

3

"A good start in life is as important to plants as it is to children; they must develop strong roots in a congenial soil."

~Vita Sackville-West

Let's face it: plants aren't designed to grow in confined places. Their roots are programmed to reach out in search of water and nutrients; they don't expect to be thwarted along the way by compacted soil or walls of terra cotta, plastic or wood. If we expect plants to grow and thrive during their "confinement," we must compensate. An ideal soil for containers is vastly different from good garden soil. Understanding this is an important first lesson.

Garden soil is a mix of mineral particles such as clay, sand and silt, and organic matter. It has a structure, which is how the particles of minerals and organic matter are arranged. The best arrangement, or structure, occurs when irregularly shaped and sized particles fit together so there is the optimum space for moisture and air to reach plant roots. This is sometimes referred to as "soil that's in good tilth." Undesirable extremes are too much space (as in the case of extremely sandy soils) or too little space (typical of heavy clay) between the particles. In these cases, the soil dries out too quickly or too slowly. Organic matter in soil is constantly renewed by the activities of earthworms, nematodes and other microorganisms that thrive in the decaying plant detritus present in good garden soil, and their activities also help maintain the porosity of the soil.

Garden soil is sometimes referred to as "topsoil" or "garden loam," although topsoil generally refers to the top few inches (about 7 cm) of garden soil. Bags of garden loam and topsoil sold at nurseries aren't generally sterilized, but can be used in container mixes, if desired.

Unfortunately, ordinary garden soil, no matter how healthy, rich and friable, loses many of its desirable, natural characteristics once it's confined to a container. It quickly becomes a compact, dense clod that restricts the movement of oxygen and water around plant roots in a container. Roots can't breathe, water doesn't drain freely and the plant suffers. The frequent watering that container plants require compacts garden soil until it acquires the characteristics of concrete. No matter how lovingly tended, the plants, if grown in a container filled entirely with soil simply dug from the backyard with no additional amendments, will fail to thrive.

The characteristics of good container soil include the ability to absorb water more quickly and drain more freely than ordinary garden soil and to do so without becoming dense and compacted. It should also be free of weed seeds, disease organisms, and harmful insects and their eggs and larvae.

If you're fortunate enough to have excellent garden soil right in your own backyard, you can amend it with peat moss to help retain water and improve its aeration by adding coarse sand, perlite or vermiculite (more on the amounts later). Soil can be sterilized to reduce the chance of weeds and disease. Sterilizing—also called "pasteurizing"—is a messy, smelly undertaking, however. The soil must be heated to 180°F (82°C), which means baking it in your oven. Trust me, the aroma as it bakes won't make you think of homemade apple pie.

Happily, garden centers, nurseries and hardware stores stock a plethora of commercial soil mixes suitable for growing plants in containers. All of them contain similar ingredients in various proportions to make a mix that can withstand repeated watering and maintain its structure over a long period of time. Once you know what the various ingredients do, and what different ratios will accomplish, you'll be able to make the most economical and suitable choice. Or you can buy the individual ingredients and customize a mix for your particular requirements.

Basically, there are two kinds of bagged, commercial mixes sold for container growing—one contains no soil whatsoever, and is called "soilless mix" or sometimes "seed-starting mix." A soilless mix contains mostly sphagnum peat moss, along with vermiculite and/or perlite. Some may contain gypsum or limestone. (Limestone counteracts the acidity of the peat moss to make the soil mix more neutral and therefore more suitable for growing a wide variety of plants.) The second type of container mix is usually called "potting soil," and it does contain soil—a clean, rich topsoil—along with perlite and/or vermiculite and sand. Of course, manufacturers apply all sorts of names to bags of planting media designed for container growing: "basket mix," "seed-starting mix," and "window box and planter soil."

Read the list of ingredients before buying; what's called "basket and planter mix" at one store may be entirely different from another bag sold for the same purposes at a store down the street. To add to the confusion, some packagers don't list ingredients, which is frustrating. The type of mix you use—soilless or soil-based—depends on what you're growing, the container's size and whether it's a permanent planting or a one-season wonder. Sometimes, it comes down to personal preference. Here are the characteristics of each.

 ## Soilless Mixes

Soilless mixes were first created in the 1940s at the University of California and Cornell University in New York as a way to have a standard growing medium for seeds and cuttings. They contained peat, perlite, ground bark and varying amounts of nutrients like superphosphate and limestone, depending on what plants were to grow in the mix.

Lightweight, clean and easy to work with, soilless mixes are usually more expensive than soil-based types. They offer superb water retention, yet allow excess water to drain freely. Over time, these attributes decline, especially with small amounts of mix that are watered frequently. Ironically, if a container with soilless mix dries out completely, it's difficult to rewet—bone-dry peat almost repels water. You must also be diligent about feeding plants because these mixes contain no plant nutrients. Mix in a time-released fertilizer according to package directions at planting time or use a water-soluble fertilizer when plants are growing. (See "Keeping Your Plants Well Fed" on page 34 for more information.)

Soil-Based Mixes (Potting Soil)

Lift equal-sized bags of a soil-based mix, often called "potting soil," and a soilless mix and you'll appreciate the basic difference between the two media. Potting soil contains soil, which makes it heavier. And a potting soil that uses soil with a high clay content will be heavier than a bag of potting soil based on lighter weight loam (loam is a balance of sand, silt and clay). A soil-based container mix is only as good as the soil it contains. Most potting soil formulations also contain peat moss, sand and perlite and/or vermiculite. Of course, soil offers more than weight: soil provides nutrients and minerals for the plants. Their presence serves as a buffer should too much or too little fertilizer reach a plant. Usually, if water-retaining polymers or fertilizer are included, they're listed on the package. Make note of this because you don't want to double dose by adding more polymers and fertilizer at planting time.

Often the relative weights of soil versus no soil are deciding factors. But even then it's not an easy choice—a balcony gardener may appreciate the lightness of a soilless mix, but weight isn't the only consideration. Those lightweight containers may blow over in the wind, while long-term container plantings will need the myriad nutrients and minerals that soil provides.

Which Mix Is Best?

It depends. I use a soilless mix in small containers because it remains loose and lightweight. Any mix—soilless or not—eventually packs down in a container after a several months of watering, but my small containers are replanted each spring. I also prefer soilless mixes for hanging baskets and window boxes because it weighs considerably less than potting soil. For containers larger than 12 inches (30 cm) in diameter, I use potting soil and usually amend it with soilless mix, or a combination of sphagnum peat moss, vermiculite or perlite and/or coarse sand. This is because the packaged potting soil that is sold at the nurseries and garden centers where I live is quite dense and heavy, with lots of clay. If I have a supply of good compost, I use it in place of some of the peat moss or garden soil/potting soil.

I find large containers that hold a dozen plants or those that will support plants for more than a season or two, such as containers of hardy or tender perennials I winter over, benefit from the qualities only soil and organic matter can provide. For exceptionally large containers, such as half-barrels, I fill the bottom half with regular garden soil that's been amended with a bit of peat moss or perlite (not much) and use a commercial light potting soil for the top half. Blend some of the rich top layer into the denser bottom layer to prevent a barrier that might impede roots from growing or water from draining.

Sometimes the type of container mix you use comes down to knowing what feels right, recognizing a good texture, and understanding what's compatible with your watering habits, climate, plants, pots and other variables. I keep a few bins of coarse sand, vermiculite, perlite, composted manure and peat moss on hand to amend soilless mixes and potting soils as needed. I'm sure soil scientists could fine-tune some of my recommendations, but often just getting your hands dirty is the best way to find out what suits.

 ## Making Your Own Mixes

One of the benefits to making your own container mix is that you can customize it to suit your containers and plants. And if you need wheelbarrows of mix, buying the individual ingredients in bulk and stirring up your own might be more economical. I'm not totally convinced of this, however, because bags of ready-made soilless mix or potting soil often go on sale at garden centers at the beginning or end of the season. I stock up then. Just make sure you have the space to store the ingredients and a place to mix up large batches.

Following are recipes for different mixes—try one or two to see which one you like best. If you're making a soil-based mix, you can use packaged potting soil, or, if you're lucky enough to have healthy, loamy garden soil, use it instead. When using peat moss, moisten it before mixing. It's less dusty to work with and incorporates more easily with other ingredients. Large, shallow bins or big, waterproof tarps are useful when mixing large amounts of container soil. I find a wheelbarrow the right height and size, and it has a flat bottom so I can dig down with a shovel and turn everything to mix it thoroughly.

Whether you're mixing your own or using packaged media, keep storage bins and leftover bags sealed to maintain moisture. You also don't want open bins or bags to get waterlogged when it rains.

Homemade Soilless Mixes

Soilless Mix with Nutrients
1 bushel (35 L) sphagnum peat moss
1 bushel (35 L) vermiculite or perlite
2 cups (500 mL) bonemeal
6 tablespoons (90 mL) superphosphate
6 tablespoons (90 mL) ground limestone

Basic Soilless Mix
6 parts sphagnum peat moss
1 part vermiculite
1 part perlite

Homemade Soil-Based Mix

2 parts garden soil or potting soil
1 part sphagnum peat moss
1 part vermiculite, perlite or coarse sand

Variations
For a lighter weight mix use:
1 part garden soil (instead of two)
1 part vermiculite or perlite (not coarse sand)

For big balcony containers with permanent plantings use:
2 parts perlite
2 parts vermiculite
2 parts soil
1 part sphagnum peat moss

Definitions

Bonemeal
Organic fertilizer made from ground, steamed bones left over from meat processing; contains 12 percent phosphorus.

Compost
Decomposed and decayed organic materials used as an organic amendment to improve the structure and nutrient content of soil. Also called "humus," which is probably more correct, but used less often. In Britain, compost also means potting soil. (See "Translating the British Code" on page 25.)

Gypsum
Powdered pellets containing calcium sulfate; improves aeration.

Lime or Limestone
White powder or pellets made from limestone. When mixed with magnesium, it's called dolomitic limestone. Used to neutralize or raise the pH (alkalinity) of soil; often added to mixes with a high proportion of peat moss, which is acidic.

Translating the British Code

Gardening books and magazines from Britain use a vocabulary to describe soil and soil mixes that can be slightly puzzling because some of the words mean something different to North American gardeners. Here's a translation.

Compost or Potting Compost

Usually refers to what we call "container soil" or "potting soil," not to be confused with what we dig out of our bins or piles after organic waste decomposes. It can mean either a soil-based or soilless container mix.

Loam-based Compost

A mix that contains soil; what we usually refer to as "potting soil."

Soilless Compost

A mix for container growing that contains no soil, "soilless mix."

John Innes Composts

These aren't trade names of potting mixes, but the names of formulas devised at John Innes Horticultural Institute in Surrey, England, in the 1930s after six years of experimentation. They were created to replace the myriad mixes made by local nurserymen at the time—often of wide-ranging quality—and to provide a growing medium that would give consistent results for the plant research being done at the institute. All John Innes Composts (seed-starting, No. 1, No. 2, No. 3, etc.) are a mix of seven parts pasteurized loam (soil), three parts peat and two parts coarse sand, with added fertilizer. The higher the formula number, the more fertilizer is in the compost. However, because various companies sell John Innes Composts under their own label, there are slight variations, depending on the type of loam used and the type and amount of fertilizers added.

Loam (Topsoil, Garden Soil)

Rich soil with a high quantity of organic matter and a balance of clay, sand and silt particles. Soil is classified as loam when it contains about 30 percent to 50 percent silt, 10 percent to 25 percent clay and less than 50 percent sand. If you're buying a truckload of loam or topsoil, know its source; you don't want to import trouble in the form of heavy clay, weed seeds or plant diseases.

Perlite

Small, lightweight, white pellets that look like Styrofoam, it's formed from ground volcanic rock that's heated until it expands to about 20 times its original size. It improves drainage and helps retain water. (The particles don't absorb water, but water adheres to their surface.) The more finely ground grades of perlite are less likely to float to the surface of a container. Hard and gritty, perlite is dusty when dry.

Potting Soil

Commercially packaged soil or soil mix, usually pasteurized to eliminate weed seeds and pathogens. Often peat moss is part of the mix; sometimes sand and vermiculite or perlite, and a slow-release fertilizer are added. Not all packages list ingredients. If it's heavy to lift, it probably contains mainly soil that's high in clay content.

Sand

Helps aerate mixes containing soil; improves drainage. Just like soil, not all sand is alike, and some isn't suitable for container growing. Builder's sand, play or sandbox sand, beach sand and some horticultural sand are all too fine in texture for container mixes—or for amending garden soil, for that matter. (If it passes through a window screen, it's too fine.) Sand made up of fine grains will consolidate in the mix and impede drainage, not improve it. What you want is coarse sand, sometimes called "grit" or "sharp sand." It should contain particles of various sizes and feel coarse and gritty. Look for it at lumberyards and building-supply centers. It's puzzling why garden centers and nurseries rarely stock it.

Soilless Mix (Seed-Starting Mix)

Predominately peat moss with smaller proportions of perlite, vermiculite and gypsum added to increase porosity. Highly water-retentive, it contains no nutrients and is sterile.

Sphagnum Moss

The live moss that grows on top of a peat bog. Sphagnum moss plants, usually pale green to greenish-red, have leaves like sponges that absorb up to 20 times their weight in water and clump together. It's used for lining hanging baskets.

Sphagnum Peat Moss

Derived from partially decomposed sphagnum moss and other plants in ancient bogs found in parts of the U.S. and Canada, it's usually sold in compressed cubes or bales that expand to twice that amount when water is added. Moisten thoroughly before using (lukewarm or warm water works more quickly than cold). It contains no nutrients, but holds five to 15 times its weight in water. It increases the acidity of soil (lowers the pH), more so as it breaks down—but this is not usually an issue with one- or two-season container plantings. It can be neutralized with the addition of lime, if desired.

Superphosphate

Fertilizer containing 20 percent phosphorus, it's made from rock phosphate treated with sulfuric and/or phosphoric acid.

Vermiculite

Grayish-brown flakes or chips of mica treated with heat and pressure until they expand to many times their original size. It contains some traces of calcium, potassium and magnesium, all beneficial for plant growth. Look for horticultural grade vermiculite; it has smaller particles than construction grade, which is used for insulation. Vermiculite aids water and fertilizer retention, and increases porosity in soilless and soil-based mixes. Its properties are similar to perlite, but vermiculite is slightly more expensive.

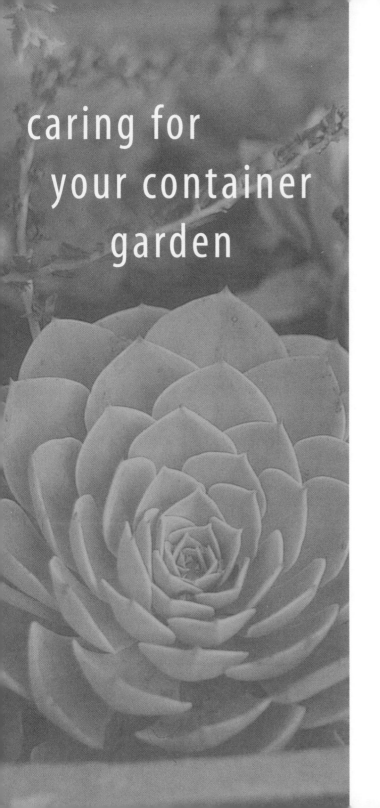

caring for your container garden

4

"The great wonder,
in gardening,
is that so many plants live."

~Christopher Lloyd

Gardeners are a demanding lot—potted gardens with less than perfect flowers and foliage spell disappointment. The right soil and healthy stock get things off to a lovely start, but without proper watering and feeding your plants will inevitably—and usually irretrievably—falter. They will flower less, grow straggly and offer scant resistance to insect pests and diseases, which are ever anxious to get a toehold in your garden. Now that you've come this far, it would be a shame not to follow through. Here's how to keep everyone happy and healthy.

Water Wisely

All plants need water to survive, but not all plants need the same amount of water at the same time. This complicates a gardener's life—how much easier it would be to mark the calendar, "Monday: water container plants." Plants growing in the open ground send feeder roots out to search for water when the nearby soil is dry. Plants in containers have restricted root growth, and their roots soon reach the sides of a pot when they go searching for a drink.

Watering containers is a fine balancing act. The limited soil in containers may dry out quickly, yet by their very nature, containers are easy to overwater, which is just as problematic. Soggy soil drives out air and kills plant roots. Plants try to be helpful and signal to us when they're water-stressed—unfortunately they give the same signal for too little or too much water. They wilt.

Naturally, it's not a good idea to wait until plants are wilting before you get out the watering can or hose. A consistent level of moisture promotes healthy plants, which means a plant is less susceptible to pests and diseases, more floriferous or productive, and better able to tolerate other stresses, such as extreme temperature fluctuations and wind.

Since watering can't be scheduled, it's up to gardeners to learn how to anticipate their plants' water needs. The size and material of the container, the density of the plants, the amount of sun and wind to which the plants are exposed, the temperature, the type of soil and individual plant preferences all affect how often and how much water is needed.

Plants growing in small containers need more frequent watering than those in more spacious quarters. A small container holds less soil, which, in turn, is less able to keep water in reserve for plant roots. Check small containers daily. On hot, sunny days, check them in the morning and late afternoon. Hanging baskets, especially those lined with sphagnum moss, may require water twice a day, too, because the soil is more exposed to the drying effects of wind.

Containers made of porous materials, such as terra cotta or fiberboard, dry out more quickly than those made from plastic, glazed earthenware or metal. To reduce the watering demands of a porous container, place a slightly

The Potted Garden

smaller plastic container inside, or line the pot with flexible plastic. Garbage or grocery bags work well; trim away excess plastic wrap once the pot is planted. All plastic liners need to have drainage holes.

Peat-based, soilless mixes dry out more rapidly than mixes containing soil such as topsoil, potting soil or garden soil. They're also more difficult to rewet once they dry out completely.

Small transplants and newly planted specimens are more dependent on regular watering, and less likely to recover from water stress than plants that have acclimatized to life in a container. Be extra vigilant of the youngsters.

When to Water

Start by looking at the soil in the container: dry soil is lighter in color than is moist soil. If it appears dry, scruff the first inch (2.5 cm) or so: if the soil at this level is also dry, the pot needs watering. A quick way to tell if a relatively small container needs watering is to lift it up: dry soil weighs less than moist. If the soil mass has shrunk away from the sides of the pot—which happens more with soilless mixes—you need to water immediately, and with greater care.

Check plants in the morning, when they're at their best. On very hot days, plants may flag in the afternoon because they're heat-stressed, not because they need water. At these times, if the soil feels moist, wait until early evening to see if the plants perk up. Another reason not to water in the middle of the day is that water sitting on leaves under the sun's glare may cause leaf scorch—the water acts like a lens, concentrating the sun's rays on the leaves. Avoid watering at night; moisture left on leaves is an invitation for plant fungi to spread their spores on the wet foliage.

If you nurture several dozen containers like I do, daily monitoring may seem a bit daunting. But after a few weeks, you become more attuned to the plants' needs, and a pattern evolves based on your past experiences with potted plants, what the weather in the preceding days has been, how quickly your particular soil mix loses moisture and how fast the plants are growing.

Don't be fooled into thinking a day of steady rain will let you off the hook. Rain doesn't reach under the eaves, pergola or porch roof where containers often congregate. And closely spaced plants within a container means there's little exposed soil surface; rain will run right off the tight canopy of leaves and on to the ground—no significant amount will make its way into the container.

How to Water

A watering can or water wand attached to a hose is best—most hose nozzles deliver water too forcefully and quickly. If you prefer to use a nozzle, invest in

Quick Diagnostics

Signs of Overwatering or Poor Drainage
- wilted, limp leaves
- moldy flowers or buds
- brown leaf tips
- young and old leaves drop off
- brown, mushy roots
- yellow bottom leaves

Signs of Underwatering
- wilted, limp leaves
- flowers that fade soon after blooming
- brown, dry edges on lower leaves
- older, lower leaves drop off

When You're Away

If you're going to be away for a few days, move as many containers as possible to the coolest, shadiest spot in your yard, and place them close together. This slows evaporation, and also makes it handier for whoever comes in to water.

Or rig up a temporary drip system for large containers. Position a pail of water next to and higher than the container to be watered, and place one end of a thick, absorbent rope or a strip of cloth in the water, making sure it rests on the bottom of the pail. Push the other end just below the soil surface. The capillary action moves a trickle of water along the cloth from the pail to the pot.

one that allows you to adjust the flow of water. I prefer a watering can because it provides more control over the amount and pressure of the water, and I consider using one a soothing ritual—administering to the thirsty—after spending a day behind my desk. A water wand is a lightweight metal or rigid plastic tube that connects to a garden hose at one end and has a spray head at the other; there's a pistol grip or shut-off valve near the hose end to regulate the flow of water. Water wands are quick and effective, too, and the best choice for hard-to-reach hanging baskets or window boxes. However, some are unwieldy, especially when water is coursing through them under high pressure, and I find anything to do with garden hoses fraught with frustration. Child-size water wands are slightly shorter and lighter than adult-size models, and easier to maneuver—perfect for uncoordinated adults. To rig up an inexpensive water wand for hard-to-reach baskets and boxes, tape a broom handle or sturdy stake to the first 3 feet (90 cm) of a garden hose and turn the water on to a slow trickle.

Other methods of delivering water to plants are drip irrigation systems, water-retaining crystals and self-watering containers. Drip irrigation systems involve linked pieces of spaghetti tubing with adjustable emitter heads that regulate the amount of water dispensed. Each pot is positioned below an emitter, and the system is hooked up to a water source and a timer. The advantage is the ability to automate the watering; the downside is that it's difficult to hide the lengths of tubing and regulate the amount of water if the pots are different sizes.

Water-retaining polymers, sometimes called "watering gels," are small white crystals that swell up into soft bits of jelly as they absorb water, up to 400 times their weight. As the soil surrounding them begins to dry out, they gradually release the water they've absorbed, thereby reducing the need to water by as much as 50 percent to 70 percent. Some mixes come with water-retaining granules, or you can buy small packages and add them to your own mix. Don't overdo it, like I did the first time I used the crystals. After I watered my pots, the crystals swelled and popped up to the surface of the containers—it looked like I had planted into bowls of clear Jell-O. I removed some of the wiggly cubes of gel (which was a waste), because I was afraid so much moisture around plant stems would cause them to rot. Package instructions include how many teaspoons (or milliliters) to use; depending on soil volume, usually about two teaspoons (10 mL) per gallon (4 L) of soil. They remain effective for several years and eventually break down into water, carbon dioxide and ammonia.

Self-watering containers have an inner pot for the plant and soil and an outer pot or reservoir that holds water in reserve. A wick bridges the two parts and pulls water up to the rootball as required. (See "When You're Away," at left, for instructions on how to make a temporary self-watering container.)

It's not a good idea to water from above, which means overhead sprinklers aren't recommended to cover off a cluster of pots, because damp foliage invites fungal diseases. Sure, rain gets plants wet, but there's no need to add to this risk. Place the watering-can spout or spray head near the soil surface, and water slowly and thoroughly. "Thorough" is one of those gardening terms that's often tossed about, but rarely explained. It means applying enough water to saturate the entire mass of soil, right to the bottom of the pot. Any excess water should easily drain away, i.e., not sit in a saucer below the pot. In the case of containers where a pot with drainage holes is nested inside one without drainage, you won't be able to see water draining out the bottom. In these cases, think about how much water you're applying—passing a watering can briefly over the top of a 20-inch (50-cm) container won't saturate the soil. After watering, poke your finger into the soil again to see if it's wet below the first few inches (about 7 cm).

If you water too sparingly, the soil dries out again before moisture percolates down to all of the roots. Shallow watering encourages plants to concentrate root growth in the top few inches (about 7 cm), making them even more susceptible to stress from drought.

Don't water in the same spot every time or you may erode soil from a portion of the roots. Apply water gently for this reason, as well. A watering can with a long, narrow spout slows down the flow of water. Short, fat spouts deliver water in a heavy gush; you might as well blast your newly planted seedlings with a garden hose. Plastic containers lighten the load, not an incidental consideration when just one gallon (4 L) of water weighs 10 pounds (5 kg). Perhaps I sound obsessive about watering by hand, but a light, well-balanced watering can makes watering a dozen pots or so a smooth, relaxing interlude in your garden.

More Watering Wisdom

Here are additional tips that will make your watering efforts even more effective.

- Plants prefer lukewarm water. A jolt of cold water straight from the tap on a hot day may damage leaves and roots. If it's practical, fill watering cans several hours before watering; this also allows the chlorine in tap water to dissipate.
- Rainwater is even better. Collect rainwater from downspouts in a specially made rain barrel or make one from an old whiskey barrel. A cover keeps leaves and mosquito larvae out. Either dip your can in from the top or install a spigot at watering-can height.
- As summer progresses, plants grow larger and their roots take up more room in the container. Containers dry out much more quickly at this stage,

Mulch Matters

Just as a layer of mulch on your beds and borders helps retain soil moisture, mulching containers accomplishes the same thing. Mulching small containers where lots of flowers and foliage cover the soil surface isn't necessary, but for large containers—especially single-stemmed plants like standard roses or rosemaries, or trees—a mulch is efficient and attractive. Organic mulches such as shredded bark, cocoa bean shells or finely shredded leaves work well; bark chips and nuggets are too bulky for container use. Pea gravel or polished pebbles are attractive choices, too. I use these at the base of rosemary and bay standards. A stone mulch provides a clean, spare look to these Mediterranean herbs.

and those you usually watered once every two or three days may now need daily ministrations.

- Soil mixes that contain a lot of peat shrink when dry; they're also difficult to rewet at this stage because the water runs down between the soil and the inside wall of the pot without saturating the mix. Place the container in a wide, deep saucer or in a pail filled with lukewarm water for about 30 minutes. When the soil surface darkens, the soil is saturated.
- Don't let pots sit in standing water. If a plant saucer is still full an hour after watering the container, empty it.
- Plants usually require less water after a string of gray, overcast days. They also require less water when the days begin to shorten in fall.
- The shape of containers affects evaporation. The same amount of soil in a wide, shallow pot dries out more quickly than soil in a taller pot with a narrow opening.
- Don't make the mistake of overwatering your plants to relieve your guilt for underwatering them. Not only will the plants need to manage the effects of drought, they'll need to cope with the stress of overwatering, too.

Keeping Your Plants Well Fed

Plants can survive without food longer than water, much like we can. However, it doesn't take much time before container-grown plants begin looking for their next square meal, mainly because they quickly deplete whatever nutrients are in the small amount of soil in their containers. Plants in a garden or in nature grow in soil made up of minerals and microscopic organisms that provide the sustenance they need to survive and thrive. Their roots are able to range freely, consuming what they need, and nature's recyclers—microorganisms, earthworms and other critters—are constantly digesting decaying plant material and producing fresh organic matter to keep plants well fed.

Nutrients in a soil mix are soon leached out by the frequent watering containers require. And some planting mixes contain no real soil at all. They consist of peat moss, vermiculite or perlite and, sometimes, coarse sand, none of which contains nutrients. Their main job is to retain water, yet allow it to drain freely. Some packaged container mixes do come with fertilizer added, but not enough to get plants through an entire growing season.

So it's up to you to keep your potted plants well fed if you want to enjoy a long, productive show of flowers, fruit and foliage. Fortunately, there are products on the market that provide a quick hit of nutrients or release food on an as-needed basis. Unlike watering—which is sometimes a daily event—dinnertime for plants can be once a week at most or as infrequent as two or three times a season for trees and shrubs in permanent planters.

Basic Food Groups

First, a refresher course on the main nutrients plants need and how plants use them. When you know the contribution each nutrient makes, it's easier to figure out what a flagging plant requires. Technically, plants make their own food through photosynthesis, a process that draws on sunlight, water and carbon dioxide to produce carbohydrates. Nutrients come into play during this process—primarily carbon, hydrogen and oxygen (which come from water and air). Plants also use nitrogen, phosphorus and potassium, which organic or synthetic fertilizers provide when the soil has an inadequate supply.

Organic fertilizers are made from natural sources—plants or animals. Synthetic fertilizers are made from nonliving sources—manufactured products. Generally, organic fertilizers are slower acting than synthetics and aren't water soluble, which makes using them in containers less desirable. The exceptions are fish emulsion and liquid kelp (seaweed extract) products, which are diluted in water. I generally use water-soluble synthetic fertilizers for my container plants because I demand a lot from them in a short period of time; I reserve organic fertilizers, such as bloodmeal, composted manure and bonemeal, for plants in my garden.

Fertilizer labels list the ratio of nitrogen, phosphorus and potassium by their chemical symbols: N, P and K (here's why you needed to memorize the periodic table in high school chemistry). The order in which the elements are listed is always the same. When I first encountered fertilizer labels I had trouble remembering the order of the last two nutrients: was it potassium then phosphorus or the reverse? When I noticed they were in alphabetical order, I was able to keep them straight.

Nitrogen fosters green leaves and stems. Phosphorus promotes the development of roots, flowers and fruit, while potassium helps plants resist disease and environmental stresses, such as harsh winters, as well as encouraging the production of fruits and flowers. All plants need these nutrients, but in varying degrees. Container plants—in fact most plants, with the exception of turfgrasses—require a lesser amount, or an equal amount, of nitrogen. The numbers on a fertilizer label—10-10-10, 5-10-5, 20-20-20, for example—indicate the percentage by weight of each of the three nutrients. Therefore, a fertilizer labeled 5-10-5 contains 5 percent nitrogen and potassium and 10 percent phosphorus. A 20-20-20 plant food contains twice as much of the big three as a 10-10-10 formula does. These last two formulas are called balanced fertilizers because they contain equal amounts of each nutrient.

Feeding Options

Fertilizers come in three forms: fast-acting powders and liquid concentrates that are mixed with water and applied at regular intervals throughout the season, and slow-release granular forms added to the soil at planting time, which are effective for three months or more (check the label). Don't use the dry, powdered synthetic fertilizers designed to be dug into flowerbeds and vegetable plots for your potted garden. In the small environment of a container, these granular fertilizers dissolve quickly and deliver too heavy a dose. In a garden setting the surrounding soil acts as a buffer, but container mixes contain little or no soil. The coatings on slow-release products, which also go into the soil dry, slow the process considerably; water and/or temperature are the triggers. Slow, or timed-release, fertilizers are often used when planting a tree or shrub in a large container and can be scratched into the surface each year.

How to Fertilize with Finesse

You don't need to be a nutritionist or scientist to use fertilizers, but the more you understand how they work, the healthier your potted garden will be.

- Never apply liquid fertilizers—either synthetic or organic—to parched plants; you risk burning the dry roots. Water plants thoroughly prior to feeding, and keep fertilizer off foliage and flowers.
- Always follow the instructions on fertilizer labels and measure accurately. Just as you can drown a plant with too much water, it's also possible to overfeed a plant. Synthetic fertilizers are especially potent—too much too often will prevent a plant from absorbing water, and may kill it. Signs of over-fertilizing are leaf-tip burn and eventual plant collapse. You might also notice a whitish crust on the soil surface, which is a buildup of fertilizer salts. If you suspect an overdose, flood the soil with water to quickly dilute the buildup and then flood again to leach the salts out of the soil.
- Experiment with dosages and fertilizer types to find a regime that works best with your schedule and plants. I use either a water-soluble 10-10-10 or 15-30-15, diluted by half, every other week. Diluting by half is relatively simple: take two same-size watering cans, mix one container at full strength, following the measurements given on the package, stir the mixture and then pour half of it in the second can. Then fill each to the top with plain water. Some people prefer weekly doses, and dilute by one-third or one-quarter.
- If your plants remain in containers outdoors year round, don't fertilize them after early August. New growth late in the season won't have time to harden off before freeze-up.

Overleaf: There's no rule that says fall containers must always be filled with chrysanthemums. Here, a large concrete container is filled with tightly packed white and rose ornamental cabbages, interspersed with a few knobby fruits of the osage-orange tree (*Maclura pomifera*) and heads of burgundy cauliflower. A thick veil of English ivy circles the edge.

Right: Alpine plants are well-suited to ▶ containers—their water and fertilizer requirements are minimal, and most can overwinter outdoors in cold climates if the soil drains freely. A gravel mulch keeps water from collecting around the plants' crowns.

◀ Perennials with attractive foliage are excellent candidates for containers. The contrasting colors and textures of a plum heuchera, silver *Santolina chamaecyparissus*, scalloped lady's mantle (*Alchemilla mollis*) and spiky blue oat grass (*Helictotrichon sempervirens*) provide as much visual interest as a combination of annual flowers might.

Opposite page: Herbs and ▶ vegetables growing in containers near a kitchen door are convenient at mealtime. The plastic-lined wicker basket holds golden oregano, variegated sage, rosy trailing lobelia and one "Tiny Tim" tomato plant, a compact variety that yields plenty of fruit. Rosemary fills the galvanized tub.

Right: Burgundy pansies, variegated ▶ coleus, gold bidens, salmon million bells (*Calibrachoa* cv.), 'Gartenmeister Bonstedt' fuchsia, maroon New Zealand flax (*Phormium* cv.) and variegated vinca vine filled the brown urn at the author's front door one summer. The combination changes with the seasons—sometimes primulas, tulips and ranunculus in spring; asters, pansies and ornamental cabbages in fall; and cut boughs and branches in winter.

◀ *Left*: The elegant details and form of this shallow urn are highlighted by a thoughtful selection of foliage plants: burgundy coleus, English ivy and bright green, lacy ferns. The plants have similar cultural requirements: full to partial shade and soil that's consistently moist.

choosing and combining plants

5

"Nature writes.
Gardeners edit."

~Roger Swain

The pure joy of gardening is found in the plants we grow. Surrounding our-
selves with our favorite colors, fragrances and textures is easily done with
container gardening. Annual flowers are probably still the most popular
choices today, but many stunning containers now include perennials, bulbs,
ground covers, herbs, vegetables, fruits, shrubs, trees and vines—even water
plants. There are no right or wrong plants for containers other than those that
prefer growing conditions that we can't provide. This may be at odds with the
flower and foliage fashionistas who issue new lists of the "Ten Best Plants for
Containers" every year. Ignore those lists. Grow a plant because you like it,
not because it's fashionable, safe or easy, or because it's what the neighbors
grow or it's what you planted last year and every year before that.

That's not to say that by simply planting the flowers you like, beautiful
results are guaranteed. Sometimes you'll be disappointed with a combination
of plants that turns out to be ghastly and gaudy or—worst of all—blasé and
boring. The first annuals I ever planted together were bright orange marigolds
and pastel pansies—a dreary duo. Later, when I thought I was ultra-sophisti-
cated, I filled a container with three kinds of white flowers. The effect was ho-
hum because all the plants sported small, daisy-shaped flowers. Sometimes
you may create a container that's at odds with the rest of your garden design
and it looks out of place. This section explains design and color theories,
because it's important to understand how these theories work before you can
decide if they should be tossed aside in favor of flaunting convention.

Putting these theories into practice can be tricky because plants grow and
change as the season progresses. A large pot or window box planted with a
dozen or so small transplants in late spring will look quite different a month
later when the plants have filled out. The ability to visualize how a container
will look when plants reach their full potential comes with experience, but
here are a few guidelines to keep in mind if you're not quite there yet.

If you look at photos of gardens from 40 or 50 years ago, most containers
(if there even were any) featured a combination of what I call the Big Three:
geraniums, petunias and marigolds. Trailblazers might have snuck in fuchsia
or English ivy. Even the now-ubiquitous impatiens wasn't on the scene: it
didn't become a popular bedding and container plant until the late 1960s.
Breeders and hybridizers continued to add to the variety of plants by developing more colors and sizes of old standards. As the variety of plants available exploded, our gardens became more varied, but container plantings
seemed to evolve only incrementally—there were still plenty of potted geraniums and dracena spikes lining front steps in the '70s and '80s. I credit floral
designers for expanding our horizons. As the economy boomed, they began
using their talents on outdoor tableaus—their customers not only wanted
beautiful indoor floral arrangements, but gorgeous planted arrangements for

their patios, decks and terraces, too. Containers were a logical place for floral designers to show their artistry, and they began concocting large, sumptuous combinations of non-traditional container plants. The creativity bar was raised in other ways as well. Hanging moss baskets and half-barrels began appearing on neighborhood streets (thanks to community beautification efforts) and more entrances of public buildings were being flanked with large, dramatic containers of flowers and foliage. Container gardening had definitely grown up.

First, Consider the Containers

Choose plants that have an appropriate size and shape for the container. For example, tall flowers such as mealycup sage (*Salvia farinacea*) or spiky ornamental grasses emphasize a tall, elegant container. Conversely, a wide, shallow bowl planted with low-growing plants, such as portulaca or hens and chicks (*Sempervivum tectorum*) is a pleasing partnership. A classic urn has vase-like, graceful lines that are complemented by arrangements that almost erupt from the top. A collection of graceful plants that arch up and out, such as ornamental grasses, miniature daylilies, fuchsias and licorice plant (*Helichrysum petiolare*) mimic these lines. The above examples of plant and planter pairings emphasize the shape of a container and draw attention to it, which is the desired effect. You don't want visitors to pass right over your containers without noticing them. Rarely does subtlety have a role in container design. The more extreme or exaggerated the shape of the plants and the container, the more dramatic the effect. Picture tall, thin galvanized steel flower buckets planted with very narrow-leaved, upright, ornamental grasses. Such a bold look would enhance a modern or minimalist house and garden.

Containers in more basic shapes made with unadorned materials such as terra cotta, wood and concrete provide a neutral backdrop, and they offer the most flexibility, adapting to a variety of color schemes. Simple designs work equally well with formal and informal, luxurious and conservative settings. My collection of containers consists mostly of plain terra cotta—the material blends with the orange-red brick of my house. The largest pots are clustered on either side of broad steps that lead from the kitchen door to a large patio. Usually, the color scheme echoes the colors in the perennial borders that ring the patio and back garden—purples, blues, white, silver and pale yellow. The largest containers include a mix of plants and colors; the smaller ones hold just one kind of plant, a repeat of one that's included in the big pots. I'm not as disciplined design-wise as I could be: there are usually five or so color "experiments" scattered about where I try new (to me) color combinations.

Highly decorated containers or those with unusual, complicated shapes look best with simple plantings: one type of flowering plant, or a combination of foliage plants—ornamental grasses, boxwood (*Buxus sempervirens*) or perhaps a collection of herbs.

A basic guideline when you're selecting a combination of different plants or several of one kind for a container is this: the more ornate, detailed or fussy the container, the better it will look if it's set off with simple, less complicated plants.

Do a Background Check

Just as you need to consider the design and color of the containers the plants will be displayed in, think about the backdrop behind the container of plants. If your containers will be clustered at the base of flowering shrubs or in front of a flower border, or around a pool with chairs, table, awnings and other details, simple plant combinations or containers planted with one kind of plant are most effective. A plain background, such as a porch pillar, window or ivy-covered wall, sets off a container filled with different colors and flower shapes.

Formal or Informal?

Types of plants and how they're displayed can reinforce the formal or informal design of a house or garden. Symmetrical, geometric plantings and container placements are formal and more tailored. For example, two clipped boxwoods in matching containers, one on either side of the beginning of a path, or designs restricted to one or two colors and few plant types are decidedly formal. Asymmetrical groupings, such as three or five various-sized containers that are planted with several kinds of flowers and clustered together beside an entrance project a more casual, relaxed mood. Plants spilling over the edge of containers, weaving together and basically having their own way are informal; a standard rose (a rose grafted or pruned to resemble a small tree) or a tall urn filled with bold canna lilies is more formal. Don't be afraid to contrast styles to create surprise or emphasis, but remember, it takes moxie to mix several styles together in a small space.

Viewed from Afar or Up Close and Personal?

A wicker basket overflowing with lilac, rose and white annual candytuft (*Iberis umbellata*) is simple to create and makes a charming vignette on a table next to a wooden bench or in the center of a patio table. But its charm is greatly reduced if viewed from afar. If you want the window boxes, hanging baskets or urns on your front porch to have an impact from the sidewalk, use boldly shaped flowers and foliage. One of the most striking examples I've seen of this principle were two large black cast-iron urns flanking the front steps on an old-fashioned porch, each planted with a large snake plant (*Sansevieria trifasciata*), more often used as houseplants. The thick, sword-like foliage stood at sharp attention, almost like green sentries on either side of the front door. Simple, bold and definitely noticed. Incidentally, the use of the cast-iron urns on an old-fashioned porch is also a good example of mixing styles (formal pots, informal porch) effectively.

Contrast Plant Textures and Shapes

Mixing different plants in a container is akin to creating a mini flower border, with many of the same criteria. Choose plants with similar light and water requirements. Try to visualize what plants will look like together, taking not just their color but also size and texture into consideration. Contrasting plant characteristics adds interest to a design and can be accomplished by contrasting colors (blue and yellow, for example), plant shapes (densely packed spires of snapdragon and the spreading branches of petunias) or leaf types (shiny hostas and fuzzy licorice plant). Contrasting the shape, size and texture of leaves and flowers provides a more elegant, subtle effect than a container filled with several contrasting flower colors. The phrase "a riot of color" was coined for a reason.

It is possible to have too much contrast, and in this case the effect can be unsettling. Mixing divergent container styles—wicker baskets filled and pastel miniature roses and black cast-iron urns filled with bold cannas—in the same garden space creates a slightly discordant mood. However, this may be exactly the effect you want. Remember, the saying "Beauty is in the eyes of the beholder" was also coined for a reason.

Scale is a design term that refers to how different sizes relate to one another. A design is in scale—or in proportion—when plants fit well together. Think of a forest with tall trees, an understory of shrubs and smaller trees, and finally the flowering plants and ground covers below. A gradual staggering of plant heights is pleasing: think of a tall castor bean (*Ricinus communis*) in a large pot surrounded by short marigolds. How much better the composition would look with a few dahlias to bridge the gap between the short marigolds and tall castor bean. However, a tall standard rose with a carpet of English ivy (*Hedera helix*) circling the base of the plant is a lovely sight, too, and a good example of how knowing when to break the rules makes sense.

Make Color Work for You

Color works in mysterious ways. Used wisely, it can create special effects that make a collection of plants greater than the sum of its parts. Used haphazardly, the results are too boring or too jarring to look at.

Mother Nature doesn't have a color consultant, and she manages just fine, but we're sometimes flummoxed when it comes to choosing what goes with what. Entire books are devoted to color theory—what our eye really sees as opposed to what we think we see, how colors affect our moods and our perception of space. There's no reason to spend sleepless nights wondering if the mauve diascias go with the yellow marguerites (*Argyranthemum* cultivars)—if you like how they look together, that's all that matters. But if you've ever wondered why blue flowers look more vivid when placed next to orange than they do beside purple or red blooms, or if you've ever aimed for something with oomph, but instead created a yawn, here are some tips for using color effectively.

Color Tips

When using more than one color in a container, let one color dominate and use lesser amounts of the other(s) to accent and support it. Your eye will be easily led through the planting. For example, if you plant equal amounts of blue and white flowers, neither will register in a significant way—your eyes will jump from blue to white to blue again, unable to enjoy the composition as a whole. Instead, they'll perceive the two equal parts (the colors) as separate entities.

Sometimes we want the elegant, simple look of one color, which is called a monochromatic scheme. To keep it visually interesting, vary the flower shapes and sizes. For example, verbenas, geraniums and fuchsias can be found in clear shades of pink, and each has differently shaped blooms. Conversely, if you're using a variety of divergent colors, consider using the same plant shape to tie them all together: yellow marguerites, blue kingfisher daisies (*Felicia amelloides*), pink gerberas—all have daisy shapes.

Bright colors—red, gold, orange—are active, lively and warm. They fill up an area and appear closer than they are. Cool colors are restful, soothing and receding. If you have a long, narrow patio or balcony, placing a container filled with bold, bright bidens, chartreuse coleus and coral geraniums at one narrow end will make that end appear closer, thereby visually foreshortening the patio. If you want to accentuate a long vista, place a container at the farthest point and plant it with soft blues, creams and grays—a blue-leafed hosta, white snapdragons, heliotrope and silvery lamium, for example—and it will seem even farther away.

Sun and shade affect how certain colors look, too. Pastel yellows, pinks, blues, lilacs and white are complemented by soft, misty overcast skies (so

Spin the Color Wheel

Reproducing the color wheel is de rigueur in most garden design books. I've stared at that segmented circle of colors hundreds of times, and it still fails to enlighten me. Basically, colors that share common hues (purple and pink both share red) are more restful together than mixing complementary colors, which are opposites on the color wheel. Complementary colors provide the greatest contrast and create a dynamic that can be punchy and powerful. Red and green, orange and blue, yellow and violet are color pairings that are complementary, i.e., high in contrast.

Pure colors (bright red, yellow or violet) are easier to digest and consequently more effective in small doses than are tints, or paler versions, of these colors—pink, lemon-yellow or mauve. Usually, the most satisfactory color schemes have more of a paler or duller color and less of the brilliant, pure colors.

In the end, it's experimentation and experience that offer the most guidance. Color choice is a personal statement based on personal preferences. If you like it, that's all that matters.

common in England and on the west and east coasts of North America). These same colors would wash out under the strong sun during a Canadian prairie or American midwest or southwest summer. Rich, vivid reds, golds, oranges and purples glow in bright light. Think about your predominant climate and whether your container plantings will be displayed mainly in bright, direct light, or in shadier spots.

White isn't always the answer. People faced with a color dilemma ("Uh, oh. The orange daylilies and hot pink petunias clash.") think injecting some white flowers into the scheme will cool things down. Frankly, white doesn't always mitigate clashing colors; instead, it highlights the contrasts. If you want to plant a variety of colors in a large container but are afraid the overall effect might be too chaotic, add more foliage plants or include ivory flowers or gray-leafed plants. These are more neutralizing than bright white.

The color white shines—literally—at twilight and on moonlit nights. White glows in these light conditions, as all other colors fade in the encroaching darkness. The effect can be magical if you plant masses of white flowers near tables and chairs or along a path to the gazebo. Many white flowers are fragrant, too, such as regal lilies (*Lilium regale*) and *Nicotiana alata*. If you use your garden mainly at night, white and other light colors are best.

One of the easiest ways to decide what plants to mix together is to follow a method called "color echoes," created by U.S. garden writer Pamela Harper. "A color echo is the repetition of a color as a means of creating unity, serenity, interest and charm in a garden," she wrote in *Color Echoes: Harmonizing Color in the Garden*, a wonderful book full of easy-to-understand theories and clear examples. Basically, the theory hinges on repeating colors or highlighting the secondary color in a flower. For example, if you're using a mass of yellow pansies with burgundy faces, highlight the burgundy with a few burgundy tulips. Or highlight the purplish stems and leaves of 'Gartenmeister Bonstedt' fuchsia with purple fountain grass (*Pennisetum setaceum* 'Rubrum'). Harper suggests diluting the harshness of a strongly colored flower with one of a paler tint: hot pink geraniums combined with paler pink verbena present a more coherent picture than hot pink geraniums surrounded by stark white verbenas or purple verbenas.

Practical Matters

Naturally, practical considerations come into play when choosing plants. Assuming you know where the containers will be placed, study the sun/shade patterns in the area. Although you can compensate for less than ideal situations by shifting pots to increase or decrease the amount of sun they receive, you'll have more reliable results if you match a plant's light requirements as closely as possible. It's easier to grow shade lovers such as impatiens and coleus in sunny conditions if you plant them in large containers where soil insulates against the heat and keep them well watered; sun lovers like morning glories and cosmos don't fare as well in shady spots and produce fewer blooms than they would if grown in full sun. And it makes sense to combine plants with similar water requirements, too: impatiens and sedums in the same pot won't last long.

Also think about the amount of time you have to spend on your collection of container plants, beyond the regular watering and feeding they require. Some plants need frequent deadheading, staking or pruning. For example, regular petunias need deadheading almost daily, and a good trim in mid-summer to keep the plants stocky and full of flowers. If you don't thoroughly deadhead sweetpeas, and to some degree, pansies, they'll stop flowering.

If You're Still Not Sure

If you find yourself spending too much time wondering what plants go with each other, there's an easy solution. When I'm feeling especially pressed for time, or uncreative, I take three or five large containers of different sizes and mass one type of flowering or foliage plant in each. Then I group them in various ways throughout the summer. The overall effect is like a small border with drifts of flowers.

Many plants, especially those with distinctive characteristics, are best appreciated when grown by themselves in a container. Grasses, hostas and other foliage plants, as well as those with intricate flowers such as lilies and pansies, can speak for themselves and don't always need companions.

Annuals or Perennials?

Flowering annuals are often the mainstay of container gardens. The good soil, and regular feeding, watering and deadheading, agree with them, and most grow vigorously in a container environment. Don't be surprised if the impatiens in your planter grows to a larger diameter and height than the identical variety planted in your garden.

Other kinds of plants, such as tender and hardy perennials, spring- and summer-flowering bulbs, herbs, vegetables, water plants and woody plants, offer interesting design possibilities, too. Tender perennials and many summer-flowering bulbs won't survive cold winters, but will live on if wintered over indoors. Sometimes, it makes more sense to simply treat these as annuals and replace them next year, especially if you have limited growing space and low light conditions indoors. However, if you want to save your favorite passionflower or caladium for next season, guidelines for wintering over these types of plants begin on page 129. Likewise, you may not want to winter over the hardy perennials in your container plantings. But there are ways of saving these plants too, from one year to the next, either by moving them into a more protected area or transplanting them into the garden. (In some climates and the right container, hardy perennials may require no extra protection.) When transplanting hardy perennials into the garden, do so in early fall to allow time for new roots to grow before hard frost hits. For more information on overwintering hardy perennials in cold climates, see page 132.

How Many Plants?

Knowing how many plants you'll need to fill a container is difficult to judge. Most people, when they first start planting containers, don't use enough. The plants eventually grow and do fill in, but for the first few months, the pot looks half finished. Unless you're growing vegetables, the purpose of growing plants in containers is purely decorative, and the creations are temporary. Instant performance is called for: space plants much more closely than is recommended. This may seem counterintuitive, but your diligent watering, feeding, pruning and deadheading, combined with a clean, light growing medium, will help mitigate the tight growing quarters, and the plants will provide you with a generous exuberance. Pack in the plants and be prepared to pull some out if things get out of hand. It's far better to have two or three dynamite creations than to stretch your plant budget to barely fill four or five containers and be disappointed.

Naturally, common sense plays a role, too. If you're using fast-growing annuals at the beginning of a long summer, you can cheat a bit and plant not

Plant Combinations

Here are some suggestions for large planters (more than 16 inches/41 cm in diameter) that use a variety of foliage and flower colors.

Rich Reds, Bronzes and Purples

- Deep rose geranium with greenish bronze leaves; red-flowering lotus vine (*L. berthelotti*); crimson 'Empress of India' nasturtium; a red flowering maple (*Abutilon* cultivar) with yellow variegated leaves

- Dark burgundy coleus; chartreuse sweet potato vine (*Ipomoea batatus* 'Marguerita'); hot pink, small-flowered fuchsia; variegated trailing creeping Charlie (*Glechoma hederacea variegata*); hot pink geranium with green and white variegated foliage

- Small purple ornamental cabbages (*Brassica oleracea* cultivars); red *Pentas lanceolata*; burgundy 'Vera Jameson' sedum; pink diascia

- Gold dahlia; 'Bronze Beauty' ajuga; black-eyed Susan vine (*Thunbergia alata*); purple fountain grass (*Pennisetum setaceum* 'Rubrum')

- Trailing purple petunia; Swedish ivy; yellow bidens; purple trailing lobelia; hot pink geranium; scarlet geranium; blue Swan River daisy (*Brachyscome iberdifolia*)

Dramatic and Elegant

- Black pansies; silver dusty miller; purple culinary sage (*Salvia officinalis* 'Purpurascens')

For the Shade

- Fern; small hosta; white astilbe; 'Rainbow' ajuga (white, bronze and green leaves); 'Palace Purple' heuchera; shell pink impatiens

- 'June' hosta (small lime-green hosta with green edges); black lilyturf (*Ophiopogon planiscapus*); 'Bronze Beauty' ajuga; Labrador violets (*Viola labridorica*)

Bright and Bold

- Red canna; 'Lime Green' nicotiana; burgundy perilla (*Perilla frutescens crispa*); scarlet geranium; red trailing verbena

- Red nasturtium; gold bidens; red-flowering lotus vine; dark blue 'Victoria' salvia; licorice plant

---

quite so densely. This saves money in plants, not an insignificant consideration if you're planting a dozen window boxes. Some plants fill out as they grow up, too. For example, a 14-inch (36-cm) pot holds eight mealycup sage (*Salvia farinacea*)—tall, slender plants—but only five or six flowering tobacco plants (*Nicotiana* cultivars), which have wide rosettes of leaves at their base. If you're filling a container with an assortment of perennials, vines and foliage plants that come in four- or six-inch (10- or 15-cm) pots, space the rootballs close together and go crazy. In container gardening, less is definitely not more.

 # Buying Good Plants

It's important to start with healthy plants to help your container garden reach its full potential earlier in the season. Healthy plants bounce back faster after the inevitable traumas they encounter when moving from their small, temporary cell packs or pots to roomier quarters. Healthy plants also have more resources to muster if they need to thwart pests or diseases.

- Burgundy coleus with lime-green picotee edge; purple heuchera;'Limelight' licorice plant; Peaches and Cream' verbena

- Scarlet nasturtium; gold bidens; red, orange and gold African daisies (*Arctotis* cultivars); orange gazanias

- Large gold African marigolds (pom-pom shape); red French marigolds (smaller single blooms); bronze-and-green coleus; black-eyed Susan vine; yellow marguerite daisies (*Argyranthemum* cultivars); red salvia (*S. splendens*)

- Yellow dahlia; yellow-and-red pansies; gold variegated euonymus; lemon thyme; yellow variegated English ivy

Cool and Soothing
- Scented geranium with variegated leaves; white Kingfisher daisies (*Felicia amelloides*); purple 'Homestead' trailing verbena; licorice plant

- Magenta trailing petunias; purple heliotrope; white and pink Swan river daisies

- Blue Swan river daisies; lemon yellow snapdragons; white petunias; yellow dahlberg daisies (*Thymophylla tenuiloba*); green-and-white striped ornamental grass, such as bulbous oat grass (*Arrhenatherum elatius bulbosum* 'Variegatum')

- Silver dusty miller; white bacopa; blue 'Victoria' salvia; blue ageratum; purple trailing verbena

- White marguerite; white geranium; blue *Convolvulus sabatius*; white trailing verbena; marbled or white-edged English ivy

- White lilies; pink marguerites; lavender

- Pale lavender petunia; white browallia; silver artemisia or dusty miller; blue 'Victoria' salvia

- Pale blue and cream pansies; gold violas; bidens; lilac trailing lobelia; pale pink, small-flowered fuchsia; white trailing verbena

- Pink trailing verbena; white and blue osteospermums; pink diascia; variegated Swedish ivy; white petunias

Healthier doesn't necessarily mean larger or more mature. Sometimes older, larger plants take longer to recover from transplanting or they may be potbound, which slows a plant's growth. However, you need to balance these considerations with the desire to have full, lush containers as soon as possible after planting. Therefore, you may want to use plants in four-inch (10-cm) or larger pots, rather than plants that have spent too long in cell packs. Larger plants are also preferred for spring or fall containers, which will have shorter runs.

When buying plants grown in cell packs (shallow, plastic rectangles divided into four or six sections), look for stocky, well-branched plants with flower buds, not full-fledged flowers. Plants already in bloom in these small cells are expending a lot of energy, which you'd rather they expend after they're planted in their permanent location. If you're concerned about getting exactly the right color of pansy or petunia, find a flat that has a few specimens in bloom just to verify that it's the color you want. Don't rely on labels because the plant tables at garden centers in early spring are chaotic, and labels get jostled into the wrong spot.

Take a pass on tall, gangly plants, or those with dull, grayish leaves. They've probably been stressed by drought or crowded growing conditions, been deprived of light for too long or experienced sudden extremes in temperature during transport from the wholesale grower to the retail shop. Obviously, plants with spotted, chewed, yellowing or dropping leaves aren't a bargain, either.

Sometimes cuttings are rooted by inserting the cut end in a small cube of florist's foam, which is then planted in a small pot. Check to make sure the cube isn't half exposed and dried out; the cutting may have too few roots to sustain transplanting or may have suffered from drought.

With large plants, check the bottom of the pot. If a matted mass of roots is struggling to escape from the drainage holes, the plant has probably spent too long in a small pot, and its growth may be stunted. If this is a must-have plant, however, you can salvage the situation by running a sharp knife down the sides of the rootball, slicing it in three or four spots, before planting. This bit of tough love helps stimulate new roots to grow. Trying to untangle the root mass by hand usually creates too many jagged tears in the roots, which invite disease.

Healthy Plants—The Main Aim

Finally, any endeavor will be less than thrilling if the plants in your container aren't healthy and well cared for. A pot packed with simple yellow marigolds—all in full bloom, spent flowers removed, with bright green leaves on healthy, compact plants—is a far cheerier sight than the most artful composition of the newest horticultural darlings that have been neglected and left to fend for themselves. Getting your potted garden off to a healthy start helps, too; the next chapter describes how.

planting
a container

6

"Gardens are not made
by sitting in the shade."

~Rudyard Kipling

The empty containers you selected with care are sitting on the garage floor, an open bag of fresh potting soil next to them. Nearby are numerous plastic trays full of plants that you spent hours deliberating over at the nursery.

Now what?

This is the juncture where a great container garden—or one that's just ho-hum—comes to fruition. Great containers and wonderful plants don't necessarily mean success—the final results are determined by the way these two ingredients come together. Planting a container is like following a recipe: if you gather the proper ingredients and also follow the method, the finished dish you place on the table will be delicious. You've gathered your ingredients (containers, plants and soil mixes), and you have an idea of how you want the container to look when you're finished—but how do you get there? You can't just throw everything into a pot and hope Mother Nature will work her magic: you need a method.

The time you spend planting a container is proportionate to its expected lifespan, health and beauty. Careful planting does take a bit more time than the slam-and-dunk method, but the results are well worth it. Let me hasten to add that there's nothing complicated about planting a container. After all, plants are very forgiving beings; they want to thrive and have the physiology to tolerate less than ideal situations—drought, wind, tight quarters—but only up to a point. However, when we give them as many advantages as possible, explained below, they will surpass all of our expectations.

How to Plant a Container

Prepare the plants.
Water plants a few hours before transplanting, and allow excess water to drain away. An evenly moist rootball is easier to remove from its pot and less likely to crumble apart when you do remove it.

Choose a cloudy, cool day to plant.
Plants transferred from their cramped, temporary grow pots into their permanent new homes will be stressed, and hot, bright sunshine just adds more stress. However, if your trays of annuals have been languishing on your garage floor for a week because you've been too busy to garden, and this Saturday is the only day you have free for the next week… then this is it, even if it's hot and sunny. Sometimes, the ideal time is the time at hand.

Find your positions, everyone.
If the containers will be portable after they're filled, do your planting where it's convenient and cleanup is easy. If you're planting a big, heavy iron or stone

urn, move it into place empty, and plant on site. This may seem obvious, but I'm embarrassed to admit the number of times I've gotten carried away and merrily planted terra-cotta pots I could barely move when empty, let alone after they were filled with gallons of moist soil and plants. (And yes, I did sheepishly "unplant" them, move the empty pots, and start again, hoping the neighbors weren't watching.)

If you have a large pot that rests on a pedestal or pot feet, the same cautionary note applies. Your time will be better spent admiring your handiwork than waiting in the chiropractor's office with strained back muscles.

Prepare new terra-cotta pots.

Submerge new terra-cotta pots in water for 15 to 20 minutes to saturate the clay. An old plastic garbage bin works well for large containers. When bubbles on the surface of the pot disappear, it's fully saturated. Soaking prevents the pot from wicking moisture from the soil mix after planting. For porous pots, such as terra cotta, wicker or fiberboard, less than 10 inches (25 cm) in diameter, line them with clear or dark-colored plastic (plastic shopping bags are perfect). A plastic lining helps maintain consistent moisture levels in small pots, a boon during hot weather when you're scurrying around with a watering can. After filling the container with soil, trim away the excess plastic at the top. To provide drainage, poke a skewer or plant stake up through the drainage holes in several places, puncturing the plastic.

Clean old pots.

Remove built-up fertilizer salts with a wire brush, scrub brush or a nylon pot scrubbing square. If you had trouble with disease in last year's container plantings, sterilize pots by washing them in a solution of one part household bleach to nine parts water. Rinse well. I rarely sterilize pots because I find using fresh soil each season cuts down on all but the most virulent plant pathogens. The patina of an old terra-cotta pot with patches of mold and moss adds an air of permanence to a garden setting, so I'm not concerned with scrubbing pots until they look like new.

Avoid the great gravel myth.

If I could dispel one myth about container planting it would be the one that recommends placing a broken piece of a terra-cotta pot or a large stone in the bottom of a pot before filling it with soil. There is a mistaken belief that this practice improves drainage when it really does quite the opposite. When a pot shard sits over a drainage hole, it seals it off and actually impedes drainage. Another popular recommendation is to place a layer of gravel in the bottom of a pot to improve drainage. Unless a piece of water-permeable landscape cloth is placed over the layer of gravel, soil filters down to fill the spaces between the large pieces of gravel. Two more reasons to forgo gravel: it takes up valuable space where roots could grow in soil and adds considerable weight to the container.

Instead of using a pot shard or gravel, cut a square of plastic window screen netting larger than the diameter of the drainage hole, and place it over the opening. The netting keeps soil in the pot, lets excess water drain freely and has the added benefit of keeping sow bugs and pill bugs from crawling into the pot. (Although even with the screen, the little crustaceans still congregate on the bottom of pots, but they're rarely troublesome.) Window screen is inexpensive and readily available at building-supply and hardware stores. When emptying pots in the fall, save the squares and reuse them next year.

Add the soil mix.

Make sure you have enough of the appropriate soil mix on hand for the containers and plants you're using. It's frustrating to run out of soil when you're up to your elbows in small pots of flowers and half-full containers. Chances are if you do run out, it will be a Saturday morning in spring, when garden centers are packed. The last thing you'll want to do is fight the crowds for something as basic as a bag of soil. It's better to buy more than what you think you'll need (especially if you come across a sale) and store whatever is left over after your planting session. Just seal up open bags and use the rest next year.

Empty the bag of commercially packaged mix—or the homemade mixture you made earlier—onto a work surface or into a wheelbarrow. Break up large clumps and remove big pieces of partially decomposed wood. Add lukewarm water and mix it in thoroughly just until the mix is evenly moist—not soggy and mucky. If adding time-released fertilizer or water-retaining polymers, mix these in at this stage. Make sure you know the volume of the soil you're working with so you don't overdo either.

Scoop the soil mix into the container and press down lightly to eliminate air pockets, especially in large containers. But don't pack it down too firmly—there's no need to stomp on it or take a block of wood and jab it into a solid mass that will starve the roots of oxygen.

How much soil mix you place in a container before planting depends on the size of the rootballs going into it. If only one large plant—say a hosta or rose—is destined for your container, fill it with enough soil so that when the bottom of the plant rests on the potting mix, the top of the plant's rootball is one inch (2.5 cm) below the rim of the container. If a dozen young plants from cell packs are going into the container, fill until the soil is a little more than one inch (2.5 cm) below the top. When you plant, the soil level will rise about a half inch (1 cm). If your design includes plants with various size rootballs, plant the largest specimen first, add more soil, plant the next size up and so forth.

Plot your design.

Gather the plants you intend to use. Arrange them, still in their pots or cell packs, on top of the soil in your container. Check the spacing and the arrangement, always keeping in mind from what angle the container will be viewed. If it's against a wall, place taller plants at the back; if it will be viewed from all sides, make sure all aspects are planted evenly. Once you're pleased with your arrangement, move the plants back to the floor or table you're working from.

Remove plants from nursery pots.

Never pull a plant out of its pot by its stem. Stems, especially young ones, will bruise, and the plant's vascular system will have difficulty moving water and nutrients up to its shoots, leaves and flowers. If the plant is in a cell pack, tip it on its side and squeeze near the bottom; the plant usually pops right out.

For plants in larger plastic pots—four to six inches (10 to 15 cm) and up—place the stem between your index and ring fingers, with your palm covering the soil surface. Turn the pot upside down, gently cradling the top of the rootball in your hand. Rap the rim of the pot on the edge of a table once or twice, or whack the bottom of the pot with a trowel handle. Either action should jar the plant loose so you can slip it out of the pot intact. If the plant still refuses to budge, poke a pencil or plant stake into the drainage holes and try pushing the plant out. If roots growing out of the drainage holes are preventing the pot from coming loose, cut—don't pull—them off.

Annuals are sometimes sold in small, fiberboard trays that aren't divided into sections, like plastic cell packs. Usually there are four to six plants to a tray and the roots have grown together. Peel away the pot and cut the rootballs apart with a sharp knife, like you would a tray of brownies. Don't try untangling the roots. The tearing and pulling will damage them more than a clean cut with a knife.

When you're moving a large plant from a one-gallon (4-L) plastic pot into another container, lay the potted plant on its side (if there are branches or foliage that may be damaged, loosely tie them together with twine, or wrap them with an old sheet and staple the edges as a temporary protection against damage). Gently roll the pot from side to side, pressing on the sides to loosen the rootball. Slide the pot away and tip the plant upright. Cup your hands under the rootball (willing it to stay intact and not break apart) and lift it up and into the new container.

The aim of all this care in transplanting plants from their growpots into their permanent homes is to disturb the roots as little as possible. However, there are times when a plant benefits from a little tough love. If a plant is hopelessly potbound, usually the case in larger specimens that have remained in too-small growpots for too long, you'll need to send a signal to the circling,

How Much Soil?

When pot dimensions are listed, the measurement refers to the diameter at the top of a pot. Most standard-size pots are slightly taller than they are wide, and slightly wider at the top than the bottom. Here's a rough guideline of how much potting mix you'll need for some common sizes.

- 14-inch (35-cm) diameter: 10 quarts (10 L) soil
- 16-inch (40-cm) diameter: 13 quarts (12 L) soil
- 18-inch (45-cm) diameter: 19 quarts (18 L) soil
- 24-inch (60-cm) diameter: 13 gallons (49 L) soil
- Half-barrel: 15 gallons (56 L) soil

tangled roots that will trigger them to move out into the new soil they'll be placed in. If there are a few thick roots winding around the outside of the rootball, pull them loose, if possible, so that they can easily make their way into the fresh potting soil in their new environment, or cut them away. If the rootball is a mat of crisscrossing roots with barely any soil visible, make three or four vertical slashes along the side of the rootball, from top to bottom.

Start with the largest specimen.

Nestle the plant in the partially filled container. Add more soil, gently firming it so that there is good contact between the rootball and the soil. Make sure the plant's final position is at the same level it was originally growing at—don't place more soil over the top of the rootball or let the top portion of the rootball sit above the surrounding soil. Buried too deeply, the stem may rot, and the plant will die. Planted too shallowly, the top roots will be exposed and dry out. The major exceptions to this rule are tomato plants and clematis. Plant tomato seedlings so the bottom few leaves are below soil level; more roots will grow along this section of stem, making a more vigorous plant. Plant clematis two or three inches (5 or 7 cm) deeper than it was originally growing. This prompts a few more stems to sprout.

Once the largest rootballs are in place, move on to the next smaller size, and so forth. Monitor the level of the soil in the container: to make watering easier, you want about a one-inch (2.5-cm) space between the top of the soil and the top of the container when you're finished planting. Allow for slightly more space in a large container that will house a small tree or shrub for a balcony or rooftop and less space in a small container.

As you plant, continue to gently firm the soil to eliminate large air pockets and keep the plants from settling in at odd angles. Don't press so firmly that you eliminate space for water and air to move around the roots.

Give the plants more water.

When all plants are in place, water with a watering wand set at a fine spray or with a watering can fitted with a round or oval sprinkling head with tiny holes, known as a rose, to disperse the water gently. The plants and soil mix are already well moistened, so not a great deal of extra water is required at this point. Try not to use a garden hose, which delivers a strong stream of water that may push the soil away from the rootballs. Recheck the level of the plants in the soil mix, adding or subtracting soil if necessary.

To get newly repotted plants off to a good start, add transplanter fertilizer to the water (see "Transplanter Testimonial" on page 36). The transplanter solution triggers plants to make new roots. Without more roots, a plant won't grow bigger or more floriferous above ground. After the initial feeding with a transplanter fertilizer, don't feed again until new growth commences.

Apply the final touches.

Now is the time to do a bit of grooming. Snip off damaged leaves, and remove clumps of potting soil clinging to leaves or flowers. If annuals are leggy, pinch off their tops to force the plants to make more branches. This is difficult to do when it means losing a flower or two, but you'll have fuller, flower-laden plants if you do. If you've planted vines you want to grow upright, place the stakes, trellis or obelisk in the container at this point so you can begin tying or training the stems before they develop too much of a mind of their own. If you've decided to mulch the surface with sphagnum moss, pea gravel or some other material, apply it now. If possible, keep newly planted containers in a sheltered, shady spot for a day or two before moving to their permanent location. Transplanting, no matter how carefully executed, is a traumatic process for plants.

 ## Planting a Window Box

The same method applies to window boxes, with the following refinements.

Prepare.

If you plan to plant a new wooden window box without a plastic, metal or fiberboard liner, coat the interior with a water-repellent finish and let it dry for a few days. If you intend to grow edible plants in the boxes, make sure you use a non-toxic coating (see "Wood" on page 12). If you are using a liner, check that it fits properly. If the top edge rises above the top edge of the box, trim it, if possible. If that's not practical, use trailing plants to disguise the liner's exposed edge.

Position.

Next, decide if you're going to plant the box prior to moving it to its final position, or plant it in situ. If you're going to plant it at the window, place a plastic garbage bag or some other protective covering behind it while you plant to minimize the amount of soil and other debris that might lodge itself between window screens and windows.

Plant.

Follow the steps outlined in "How to Plant a Container" on page 50. If the window box will be seen from indoors as well, plan so the rear of the container is pleasing to look at, too. (If you can periodically turn the box from back to

Hardening Off

Plants that have led a sheltered life growing under lights indoors need to be gradually introduced to the fluctuating light, wind and temperatures found outdoors before being moved into containers. This process is called "hardening off," and takes about a week.

Plants from a nursery may need some tender care, too. Sometimes they go directly from greenhouse growers by truck to the nursery and are sold in a day or two. Ask staff if the plants you choose need to be acclimatized.

On the first day, set plants outdoors in full shade or filtered shade for one hour. The next day, leave the plants outdoors for two hours, and add an hour each subsequent day. If the plants are sun-lovers, gradually move the plants into a sunnier location as the week progresses. Monitor soil moisture carefully. Plants exposed to spring breezes and sun dry out amazingly quickly, especially young plants with small rootballs. Conversely, if the plants are subjected to a sudden spring downpour, make sure excess water can drain away easily. Don't fertilize plants while they're hardening off, but do remove spent blossoms, and gently separate vines if they get tangled up with one another.

At the end of one week, the plants are ready to go into their permanent locations. However, if it's not possible to make up your containers at this time, or the weather has turned cool, most plants can be held a bit longer. But plants kept cooped up on a garage floor for two or three weeks aren't always totally forgiving.

At the end of the season, repeat the process for plants you'll grow over winter indoors—only reverse the exposure. Before nights turn cold, begin moving the plants indoors a few hours at a time, gradually increasing the time until they're spending half of the day outdoors and the rest of the day and all night inside.

front to promote even growth, so much the better.) Tall plants, which only grow taller as the season progresses, might obscure your view or reduce the amount of light entering the room.

Most window-box plantings are a combination of mounding and trailing plants. Don't plant trailers right up against the front edge of the box; as they grow, the plants' weight may dislodge the rootballs. Instead, plant trailing plants a few inches (about 7 cm) back from the edge and allow a few of the stems to weave their way through the rest of the plants before spilling over the edge. If you're using plants that don't readily trail, such as pansies, sweet alyssum or dianthus, but you want them to spill over the edge, plant their rootballs at a slight angle, so the plants tip forward slightly.

 ## Planting a Moss-Lined Hanging Basket

Planting the sides and top of a large, moss-lined wire basket is a challenge, and a bit fiddly, but a large, multicolored sphere of flowers suspended from a tree branch or pergola is truly breathtaking. In addition to the basket and liner—sphagnum moss, wool, coco fiber matting or other natural material— you'll need plenty of plants and a fair bit of patience.

Baskets with one-and-a-half- to two-inch (3- to 5- cm) openings between the wires do a better job of keeping the moss, soil and plants in place. Also look for baskets with long, sturdy chains that fasten securely to the basket's rim. Most baskets are hung too high, and we miss much of the floral impact. You may want to rig up some kind of extension to make the chains longer or suspend the basket from a bracket attached to a wall, fence or arbor. For a large-diameter basket, make sure the bracket extends far enough from the wall so the basket hangs straight down without hitting the wall. Don't place a basket directly over a path where water will drip on people as they pass through.

Sphagnum moss is the most traditional liner, although preformed mats of wool or coco fiber have recently become more available. Any natural material that holds soil and allows you to make slits for plants to grow through will work. I've seen baskets lined with evergreen boughs—juniper or cedar, for example. Another option is a fiberboard basket fitted with a wire rim and hangers. Making planting holes in the stiff fiberboard is hard work though; you'll have an easier time if you limit planting to the top surface, and let trailing plants and vines spill over the edge to disguise the fiberboard.

The following directions are for planting a sphagnum moss basket using a wire frame. I recommend lining the moss shell partway up with a layer of plastic—a piece of dark-colored or clear plastic garbage bag works well. Moss basket purists may scoff at this little cheat, but the plastic allows you to use a slightly thinner layer of moss in the bottom half of the basket and cuts down on the amount of watering needed.

Moss baskets are usually planted with rows of plants around the sides and across the top. My instructions use three rows, or layers: the bottom (which is about two or three inches/5 to 7 cm up from the base of the basket), the middle and top. The bottom row uses the fewest number of plants because it has the smallest circumference. To plant the top and sides of a 14-inch (35-cm) diameter basket, you'll need 20 plants and at least 30 plants for an 18-inch (45-cm) one. That may seem like a lot of plants, but you want them to weave together into one glorious ball of color quickly; you don't want to wait until September for the plants to fill out.

Seven Steps to a Hanging Basket

1. Moisten the soil and plants before starting. Soak the moss in warm water; wet moss is easier to shape. Don't tear the moss apart when you immerse it; submerge it in large chunks. Swish it around, to get it uniformly wet.
2. Rest the bottom of the basket in an empty pail (a brick or two in the bottom prevents the pail from tipping) or in a heavy empty pot. The idea is to stabilize the round-bottomed basket while you plant it, yet not have the sides obscured, which would make planting the bottom row difficult.

Take a chunk of wet moss, squeeze out the excess water and place it across the bottom of the basket, pressing it down firmly. Repeat with more chunks of damp moss, overlapping the pieces slightly, to form a one-inch (2.5-cm) layer of moss midway up the sides of the basket.

3. Cut a circle of plastic from a shopping or garbage bag to cover the moss. A bit of soil in the bottom keeps the plastic in place as you trim the edges even with the top of the moss. Poke holes in the bottom of the plastic for drainage; you'll make larger slits in the plastic for plants in the bottom row to slide through later. Add moist soil mix until it's slightly below the top of the moss and plastic liner; firm slightly. Now you're ready to plant the bottom row.

4. Push apart a section of moss two or three inches (5 or 7 cm) up from the bottom of the basket, and cut a small slit in the plastic liner. Remove a plant from its container and slightly squeeze its rootball to make it easier to fit between the wires. Insert the rootball far enough so it's completely in the soil and the base of the plant is in the layer of moss. Continue around the sides of the basket.

5. Extend a slightly thicker layer of moss until it reaches the top of the basket. The middle row of plants goes in next. Insert the plants for the middle row through the moss, staggering them so they don't sit directly above a plant in the bottom row. The rootballs will be resting on top of the soil and the top of the plastic liner. Add more soil, covering the rootballs in the middle row, until the soil reaches about one-half to one inch (1 to 2.5 cm) below the top edge of the moss. You need a rim of moss at the top to act as a reservoir when watering.

6. Now you're ready to plant the top row and the surface of the basket. Place a few trailers near the outer edge and one or two more upright plants in the center. Fill the spaces in between with more plants.

7. Finally, water the basket's top and sides very gently—use a watering can or watering wand set at a fine spray. Carefully check each plant: you may need to tuck in small bits of moist moss around the base of plants if roots or soil are exposed. Trim off broken stems and pinch off spent blooms. Attach chains equidistantly around the top rim and hang the basket in a sheltered spot out of direct sunlight for a few days before moving the basket to its permanent location.

plants for the
potted garden

7

"With the possible exception of squirrels,
gardeners may be
the most acquisitive
creatures on earth."

~Thomas C. Cooper

Almost any plant will grow in a container if given enough room for its roots and the water and nutrients it needs to keep it in good health. A "good" container plant thrives in a container setting and gives us pleasure. Plants that tolerate less than ideal growing conditions, that look beautiful in bloom and out, that are disease- and pest-resistant, and that don't aspire to gargantuan proportions are good choices. Still, there are hundreds—probably thousands—of plants that meet these basic criteria. This section of brief plant profiles includes what I consider to be strong performers for containers. They aren't terribly demanding, are relatively easy to find and are generous with their foliage, flowers or fruit. Admittedly, there are others that could make the cut too, but such lists are subjective. I'm sure you will discover more on your own.

The plant list is divided into four categories based on the role the plants play in a design: specimen or accent plants; fillers and mounders; climbers and trailers; and foliage plants. Each profile describes the plant's size, color range and growing requirements, as well as what type of plant it is: annual; hardy perennial; tender perennial; perennial grown as an annual; or bulb, tuber, corm or rhizome (see "What Type Are You?" on page 61).

Flowering annuals are often the mainstay of container gardens. The good soil and regular feeding, watering and deadheading agrees with them, and they grow vigorously in a container environment. Don't be surprised if the impatiens in your planter grow to a larger diameter and height than the identical variety planted in your garden.

Other kinds of plants, such as tender and hardy perennials, spring- and summer-flowering bulbs, herbs, vegetables, water plants and woody plants, offer interesting design possibilities, too. If your potted garden exists for one summer's enjoyment, there's no need to concern yourself with a perennial's hardiness rating. However, if you intend to hold plants over for next year, you have several options to consider. Tender perennials and many summer-flowering bulbs won't survive cold winters, regardless of whether they're planted in a garden or a container, but will live on if overwintered indoors. Sometimes, it makes more sense to simply treat these as annuals, especially if you have limited space and low light conditions indoors. However, if you want to save your favorite passionflower or canna lily for next season, guidelines for overwintering these types of plants begin on page 130. Likewise, you may not want to winter over the hardy perennials from your container plantings. But there are ways of preserving these plants too. You can either move them into a more protected area or transplant them into the garden. (If you live where winters are mild, hardy perennials growing in containers may require no extra protection.) When transplanting hardy perennials into the garden, do so in early fall to allow time for new roots to grow before hard frost hits. For more information on overwintering different types of plants,

Overleaf: Sometimes the perfect container isn't found at a garden center. An old spongeware pot perched on a worn wooden ladder suits this casual country garden setting. Pink double petunias and white bacopa are planted in a plastic pot with drainage holes to allow excess water to drain away.

Right: A three-tiered wire plant stand on the ▶ author's patio displays a collection of scented geraniums in small terra-cotta pots that have been collected over time; a copper tag in each pot identifies the cultivar. The tender geraniums are overwintered indoors.

◀ *Left*: Full, lush hanging baskets and window boxes of petunias, bidens and geraniums enhance a Victorian-style porch. Abundant blooms, not a restrained color combination, is the goal. Frequent feeding, watering and deadheading keep plants productive.

Opposite page: It took ▶ imagination to see the gardening potential in a battered wooden kitchen chair. Herbs, including silver thyme, rosemary and mint, are planted in a pocket of soil held in place by a piece of landscaping fabric stapled to the chair.

Left: Front entrances are a prime location for a dramatic container or two. Choose plants with bold shapes and colors that will be easily noticed from the sidewalk or street. Bright red ivy geraniums and small yellow daisies vie for attention at the base of a tall ivy-covered spiral obelisk.

Left: The long strands of variegated vinca vine reach far down the sides of a wall and give the simply planted concrete planter much more impact. The scarlet geraniums stand out against the light gray porch.

Right: A repeating motif—in this case, gloriosa daisies (*Rudbeckia hirta*) and a few bright red branches in identical galvanized sap buckets—help lead the eye up the wooden steps to the front door.

Right: Formal architecture calls for a more formal approach. An elegant black cast-iron urn echoes the heavy black front door, while a collar of mauve and white diascia and ivy encircle an upright sago pine (*Cycas revoluta*), more often seen growing indoors with house plants.

see page 129. One more general observation: hardy perennials prefer soil-based planting mixes.

Aquatic plants, fruits, vegetables and roses for containers are described in Chapter 8, "Special Gardens" on page 102. Herbs are included in that chapter, as well, although some of the more ornamental varieties are mentioned here. Criteria for selecting trees and shrubs for containers are discussed in the chapter on balcony and rooftop gardening, beginning on page 120.

What Type Are You?

Knowing what type of plant you're dealing with gives you clues as to how it will perform in your container and what kind of care it needs. Here are basic definitions for common plant types.

Annuals

Plants that grow, bloom and die in a single season. Most annuals bloom for several weeks—and bloom quickly—which make them a popular choice for containers. Deadheading (removing dead blooms) prevents plants from going to seed, which triggers annuals to stop producing flowers. Diligent dead-heading "tricks" plants into producing more and more blooms in their pre-programmed quest to set seed. Because producing flowers over a long period of time takes energy, annuals usually have higher fertilizer needs than other types of plants.

Half-Hardy Annuals

Sometimes you'll see this phrase in a seed catalog. This means the plants tolerate cool temperatures, perhaps even a few light frosts, and grow well during the cool weather of spring and fall, usually less so in the heat of midsummer.

Hardy Perennials

Plants that die back to the ground (or go dormant) when winter arrives and put forth new growth from their roots the following spring are considered hardy perennials, sometimes called "herbaceous perennials." The word "hardy" is relative: what I consider a hardy perennial in my Canadian Zone 5 garden may not be rated reliably hardy in colder zones (Zone 4 and below). I haven't included precise ratings for the hardy perennials listed in this section because in most climates, even hardy perennials grown in containers will need some type of supplemental protection. However, to find out more precise hardiness zones, consult plant dictionaries that include zonal ratings and the Canadian Plant Hardiness Zone Map or the USDA Plant Hardiness

Zone Map, available in gardening reference books and at many gardening Web sites.

Woody or Shrubby Perennial Plants

These terms refer to plants with woody stems (rosemary, bay, roses, trees and shrubs) that don't die back over winter. Some woody perennials, such as rosemary and bay, also retain their leaves throughout the year.

Tender Perennials

Plants that are killed by cold winter temperatures in your garden, but grow year-round in their warmer native habitats, are considered tender perennials. (Sometimes, after a particularly harsh winter, I think many of my so-called hardy perennials get together and decide to declare themselves "tender," but that's another issue.) Obviously, the same flexible rules apply to tender perennials as hardy perennials, i.e., what behaves as a tender perennial in one garden might be hardy in a garden where winters are usually above freezing.

Perennials Grown as Annuals

This refers to plants, usually native to tropical climates, that are actually perennials but considered annuals in northern climates because they behave like annuals in colder climates. In cold climates, they're grown for one season and then discarded when frost kills them. Often they're labeled as annuals, but technically this is incorrect. These plants aren't grouped with tender perennials because they are usually grown from seed, difficult to overwinter indoors, and relatively inexpensive to replace next season.

Bulbs, Corms, Tubers and Rhizomes

All are variations of underground plant structures. Bulbs and corms are closely related, as are tubers and rhizomes. A bulb is a storage organ made up of fleshy scales—actually, modified leaves—that store food. A corm is a swollen, underground stem that also stores food, but is solid, and not made up of scales. Tubers are underground stems with buds or eyes, which are the points from which the stems grow. A rhizome, yet another underground stem, grows horizontally, usually near the surface. It has nodes, which is where roots form.

Accent and Specimen Plants

Accent and specimen plants are usually tall, with an interesting structure or large, dramatic flowers or foliage. Accent plants act as a focal point, drawing the eye and holding our interest to encourage us to take in the entire composition. Specimen plants usually work alone, adding a singular, bold note to a container, although they may be underplanted with something subtle to round out the picture. An accent plant usually has a supporting cast that serves to heighten the star's beauty, not distract from it. A container that uses more than one kind of strong accent plant is often discordant: each plant vies for attention, no one wins and the effect is a muddle. If you want to grow tall white lilies and cannas, plant them in separate containers where they can shine on their own. Some bulbs make great accent and specimen plants, too. Although they might not be showy for as long as perennials and annuals, when they're in full bloom, they make a dramatic statement.

~ Astilbe

Hardy perennial
Height
24 to 36 inches
(60 to 90 cm)
Spread
24 to 36 inches
(60 to 90 cm)

Long-blooming perennials with attractive, ferny foliage ranging from deep green to bronze. White, salmon, pink, rose or red blooms appear on upright plumes in midsummer. Spent flowers turn an ornamental reddish-brown, which is attractive in winter.

Requirements:

Part sun to shade; protect from afternoon sun. Don't allow plants to dry out. Extremely hot, humid summers may set plants back. Astilbe needs a large pot to reach its full potential.

~ Bear's breeches *Acanthus mollis*

Hardy perennial
Height
18 to 24 inches
(45 to 60 cm)
Spread
36 inches (90 cm)

This plant inspired the leaf design on Corinthian columns. It's grown mainly as a foliage plant, but does sport white or light lilac flowers in late spring or early summer; flower spikes can reach five or six feet (1.5 to 1.8 m). Lush, glossy, deeply lobed leaves reach two or three feet (60 to 90 cm) long.

Requirements:

Sun to part sun. Plant in a large pot; don't overfertilize. Remove flower spikes after blooms fade. Careful watering during summer prevents plants from going dormant and losing their leaves too early.

∼ Caladium bicolor

Tender tuber
Height
*12 to 36 inches
(30 to 90 cm)*
Spread
*12 to 24 inches
(30 to 60 cm)*

Arrowhead-shaped, papery leaves up to 12 inches (30 cm) long. Its intricate mottled or spotted green, white, pink or rose leaves create a bold look. One caladium in a large pot fanning out over impatiens, begonias, or small hostas offers a cool, soothing vignette.

Requirements:

Shade to part sun. Protect delicate leaves from wind. Needs constant moisture and warm temperatures. Remove insignificant flowers so the plant's energy goes to leaf production. Start tubers indoors (plant bumpy side up) six to eight weeks before the last frost; move them outdoors after the weather warms up. Feed plants with high-nitrogen fertilizer.

∼ Calla lily   *Zantedeschia* spp. and cvs.

Tender rhizome
Height
24 inches (60 cm)
Spread
12 inches (30 cm)

Exotic, glamorous blooms—usually a waxy white, sometimes dusty pink, yellow or deep purple—appear about six weeks after the rhizomes are planted in late spring and continue through most of the summer. Its arrow-shaped leaves have white spots, making this plant doubly ornamental.

Requirements:

Part sun; soil-based potting mix. Provide constant moisture, or plant in shallow water of a container water garden.

∼ Canna

Tender rhizome
Height
*18 inches to 6 feet
(45 cm to 1.8 m)*
Spread
24 inches (60 cm)

Tropical-looking plants with large leaves, sometimes striped or deep purple, and brilliant red, yellow, salmon, pink or white flowers. 'Pretoria' has yellow-striped leaves and orange flowers; 'Picasso' has bright yellow blooms with red freckles; 'Black Knight' has burgundy leaves and dark red flowers. Plant three in a large container or use just one to accent equally vivid nasturtiums, dahlberg daisies (*Thymophylla tenuiloba*), medium-tall grasses and sweet potato vine (*Ipomoea batatus*) for a hot, tropical look.

Requirements:

Canna lilies prefer full sun (part sun is okay, but there will be fewer flowers); they tolerate heat. Plant in at least a 12-inch (30-cm) pot because rhizomes grow hefty over summer. Deadhead to prolong blooms. Buy plants or start rhizomes indoors a month before last expected spring frost. Move outdoors when nights are above 50°F (10°C).

~ Flowering maple   *Abutilon* spp. and cvs.

Tender, woody perennial
Height
*24 inches to 4 feet
(60 to 120 cm)*
Spread
*24 inches to 4 feet
(60 to 120 cm)*

Bell-shaped yellow, white, pink, peach or red two-inch (5-cm) flowers grow on plants with maple-shaped leaves, hence its common name. Some hybrids have variegated leaves with white edges or yellow spots. Plants sometimes are trained as a standard; 'Moonchimes' is short enough for a large hanging basket.

Requirements:

Sun to part sun.

~ Lily   *Lilium* cultivars

Hardy, summer-blooming
  bulbs
Height
*12 inches to 4 feet
(30 to 120 cm)*
Spread
minimal

Most bulbs send up one leafy flower stem with blooms near the top.
Hybrids are more vigorous in containers than the species. Asiatic and trumpet hybrids bloom from late May through early July; flowers can face up, out or down. Colors are almost limitless in variations of white, red, yellow, orange, pink, lavender. Highly fragrant and slightly taller are the late summer–blooming Orientals. 'Casablanca', with large, pure white flowers, and 'Stargazer', white with pink edges and darker pink spots, are two beauties. Tall lilies planted on their own can look top-heavy in containers; incorporate other plants at their feet for a pleasing look. If staking is needed, be careful not to skewer the bulb in the process.

Requirements:

Full sun or morning sun with afternoon shade. Buy as started plants or bury bulbs two or three times deeper than their diameter, three or five to a pot for best display.

∼ Lily-of-the-Nile   *Agapanthus orientalis*

Tender perennial
Height
4 feet (120 cm)
Spread
24 inches (60 cm)

Tall, slender stems hold large spheres of clear blue flowers; broad, arching leaves are at the base of the plant. The striking plants, which look best by themselves in a container, are beautiful beside a pool or flanking a doorway. 'Alba' has white flowers.

Requirements:

Sun to part shade; tolerates heat and forgiving if allowed to dry out. Flowers best when slightly pot-bound. Overwinter in its pot in the basement; keep barely moist. A month before last frost, move to a sunny window indoors and begin regular watering.

∼ Montbretia   *Crocosmia* spp. and cvs.

Perennial
Height
36 inches (90 cm)
Spread
12 inches (30 cm)

'Lucifer', with its long sprays of brilliant red flowers, is a popular variety. It's terrific paired with equally vivid dahlias, zinnias and marigolds, or let it smolder with deep purple browellia and dark coleus. Leaves grow in an attractive fan shape. Yellow and orange varieties are also available. Plants multiply via underground corms. Garden-grown specimens are hardy in mild climates, but container-grown montbretia need overwintering indoors.

Requirements:

Sun to part sun.

∼ Ornamental Grasses

Many types of ornamental grasses perform well in containers and are good substitutes for dracaena spikes (*D. marginata*). Perennial grasses grow quickly and show off their graceful, mature form in one season. In fact, you may wish to confine some of the wandering, spreading perennial grasses such as ribbon grass (*Phalaris arundinacea* 'Picta') to a container to prevent them from galloping through your borders. Not all grasses are tall beauties: blue fescue (*Festuca glauca*) makes 6- to 12-inch (15- to 30-cm) tufts of blue-green soft bristles, and some of the sedges (*Carex* spp. and cvs.) fall gracefully over the edge of a pot like a green waterfall.

One of the most beautiful grasses for containers is red fountain grass (*Pennisetum setaceum* 'Rubrum', sometimes sold as 'Purpureum'), a tender perennial. The reddish-green foliage makes an arching two-foot (60-cm) tall clump; fluffy, pinkish flower spikes appear in midsummer. It looks wonderful with chartreuse and burgundy coleus, but my favorite trio is red fountain grass, ruby China pinks (*Dianthus chinensis*) and *Tradescantia zebrina* 'Purpusii', which is usually sold as a houseplant, and has bright green leaves with silver and burgundy stripes.

Requirements:

Most grasses require full sun and tolerate heat and dry soil; fertilizing isn't a priority. If you plan to overwinter a perennial grass in a container, make sure its robust root system won't split the sides of the pot.

~ Standards

"Standard" is a term used to describe a plant that has been trained, grafted or trimmed so that it has a tall, straight, single stem with foliage and flowers growing at the top. Heights vary, depending on the plant. Most standards are woody plants, although vines can be tied to a stake and the ends of the vines allowed to spill and swirl around each other at the top. Good candidates are roses, sweet bay (*Laurus nobilis*), fuchsias, marguerite daisies (*Argyranthemum*), common lantana (*L. camara*), hibiscus, geraniums (*Pelargonium*) and rosemary (*Rosmarinus officinalis*).

Requirements:

Follow the cultural requirements of the particular plant. If a standard requires permanent staking, make ties as unobtrusive as possible and match the stake color to that of the stem. If new growth starts along the stem or starts to grow at the base of the plant, pinch it out immediately. Turn plants a quarter-turn every week to maintain even growth.

Standards suit formal surroundings and symmetrical designs. If planted alone, cover the soil with an attractive mulch such as polished river stones, pea gravel or clay pellets, or plant creeping thyme, periwinkle (*Vinca minor*) or low-growing sedums or other succulents at their base. If combining with other flowering plants, make sure these don't grow so tall that they obscure the stem of the standard.

Mounders and Fillers

There are hundreds of mounding, flowering plants to choose from, and they make up the bulk of container gardens. If we consider accent plants the stars, filler plants can be thought of as the supporting cast. Mass several of the same kind in one pot or use various plants with different colors, shapes and habits to make a harmonious combination. Annuals and tender perennials bloom for most of the summer, while hardy perennials usually bloom for only three or four weeks. If your design relies on perennial flowers to carry it off, you may need to substitute other plants when the blooms fade. The perennials included in the list below bloom longer than most (or rebloom after deadheading) or have attractive leaves that add interest after flowers fade. More hardy perennials appear in mixed containers every year, a welcome respite from some of the more over-used annuals, such as geraniums, petunias and the like. But perennials usually cost more than annuals, and a planter full of them will cost more than twice as much as one filled with annuals. I include a few choice perennials in containers with good form and foliage, but continue to rely on unusual annuals and tender perennials.

～ African daisies

Height
12 inches (30 cm)
Spread
12 inches (30 cm)

Arctotis cultivars (annual), *Osteosperum* cultivars (tender perennial)

Arctotis has sunny yellow, coral, orange, red, pink or white daisies, up to three inches (7 cm) wide, sometimes with darker rings near the center. Their flowers close at night and on cloudy days, and the toothed or scalloped leaves are an attractive gray-green.

Osteosperum has white, yellow, pink or mauve showy daisies, about two inches (5 cm) across, with blue centers. Petals can be an intriguing spoon shape. The flowers close on cloudy days and in the evening.

Requirements for Arctotis:

Full or part sun; heat-tolerant, but likes cool nights. Drought-tolerant. Prefers to be tightly potted, which makes them especially suited to containers. Feed less frequently than other flowering annuals, and pinch and deadhead to promote bushiness and prolong blooming period.

Requirements for Osteosperum:

Full sun and cool temperatures. Deadhead to maintain blooming.

~ Begonia

Height, fibrous
6 to 12 inches
(15 to 30 cm)
Spread
6 to 12 inches
(15 to 30 cm)
Height, tuberous
12 to 24 inches
(30 to 60 cm)
Spread
6 to 12 inches
(15 to 30 cm)

Fibrous or wax begonias (annuals), tuberous begonias
(tender perennials)

Fibrous or wax begonias grow into stiff little buns with small pink, white or rose flowers, each centered with a prominent tuft of yellow stamens. The large, round fleshy leaves are more interesting than the flowers—bronze or a bright light green—and remain pristine throughout the growing season. The flowers on tuberous begonias come in a wider range of colors; some have contrasting shades on the edges of their petals. The large flowers can be single, double or ruffled on upright or pendulous plants. Tuberous begonias inspire serious love or loathing—some people grow nothing but tuberous begonias in their containers, while others won't let one pass their garden gate. No one can deny that the variety of colors is truly astounding—sherbet shades of apricot, raspberry and lemon are hard to resist.

Requirements for fibrous begonias:

Sun to shade; heat-tolerant. Sun turns the purple- and bronze-leaved varieties an even deeper color; those with light-green leaves need more shade. Wax begonias don't need deadheading.

Requirements for tuberous begonias:

Part sun to full shade. Winds can damage brittle, flower-laden stems, and tall varieties may need propping up; tying stems to stakes is tricky because of their soft, fleshy stems. Buy plants in late spring, or start tubers indoors about six to eight weeks before the last expected frost. Place concave side up, and barely cover with soil; add more soil as shoots grow. Plant outside after danger of frost is past and the weather is warm. Pinch off the spent blooms to maintain flowering.

~ Browallia speciosa

Perennial grown as
annual
Height
12 to 18 inches
(30 to 45 cm)
Spread
12 inches (30 cm)

Available in only two colors—white and violet-blue—*B. speciosa* are work-horses in containers and spill attractively over the edge of window boxes and hanging baskets. The flower shape is similar to nicotiana, like a flared funnel. Mix browallia with pale lilac petunias, Swan river daisies (*Brachyscome iberidifolia*), pale yellow snapdragons and silver dusty miller (*Senecio cineraria*) in a container for a casual, cottage-style garden.

Requirements

Part sun to shade; don't allow plants to dry out.

~ Butterfly flower, Poor man's orchid *Schizanthus pinnatus*

Annual
Height
12 inches (30 cm)
Spread
8 inches (20 cm)

Jewel-tone flowers reminiscent of orchids appear in clusters near the tips of stems, earning the plant it's other charming common name, poor man's orchid. I love the rich hues of schizanthus, but have difficulty keeping plants in bloom past July.

Requirements:

Full sun to part shade; rich, moist soil. Prefers cool temperatures. Plants do best when pot-bound, a desirable characteristic for containers.

~ Calendula *Calendula officinalis*

Annual
Height
*12 to 24 inches
(30 to 60 cm)*
Spread
10 inches (25 cm)

Commonly called pot marigolds in Britain, in North America the plant's botanical name, *calendula officinalis*, is also used as its common name. Across the ocean, our marigolds (*Tagetes* spp. and cvs.) are commonly called tagetes. Confusing, yes, but important to keep in mind if you're reading British gardening publications. Calendulas come in less brash shades than marigolds: lemon-yellow, apricot and cream as well as gold and orange. The flowers are soft and fluffy—and edible, too.

Requirements:

Full to part sun; prefers cool temperatures and resents droughts. Blooms may be sparse in heat of summer, but plants usually pick up when cooler temperatures arrive. Deadheading is imperative.

~ Chrysanthemum

Hardy perennial
Height
*6 to 24 inches
(15 to 60 cm)*
Spread
*6 to 24 inches
(15 to 60 cm)*

The mainstay of many fall containers, chrysanthemums come in a variety of warm golds, yellows, reds and oranges, as well as rosy shades of pink and lilac. The shapes of blossoms and petals are as varied as their colors: flat daisies, quilled petals, round pom-poms or spidery blooms. Chrysanthemums need frequent pruning to set the myriad flower buds we've come to expect from them. They only come into bloom when nights are long—greenhouse growers are adept at getting plants to bloom, and there are always plenty of budded plants available for gardeners ready to redo their summer planters for autumn.

Requirements:

Full sun or part shade. Keep moist; if allowed to dry out, plants shed lower leaves. On large-flowered types, pinch out faded blooms to make room for side buds to open.

～ Cigar flower   *Cuphea ignea*

Annual
Height
12 inches (30 cm)
Spread
12 inches (30 cm)

Small tubular blooms, usually red with black and white tips; newer selections come in soft peach and clear pink. The tubular shape and bright color attracts hummingbirds. Position the plant near the front of a mixed container so the intriguing blossoms aren't overlooked. I like the peach variety combined with terra-cotta million bells (*Calibrachoa* cultivar), salmon-and-green coleus and black sweet potato vine (*Ipomoea batatus* 'Blackie').

Requirements:

Full sun or part shade.

～ Cockscomb   *Celosia* spp. and cvs.

C. argentea (perennial grown as annual);
C. spicata (annual)
Height
24 inches (60 cm)
Spread
12 inches (30 cm)

C. argentea var. *plumosa* has fluffy plumes—almost like painters' brushes—in bright orange, red, gold or pink; *C. argentea* var. *cristata* has bizarre-looking, crested combs. Rosy-red plumed celosia complement the pink shades found in *Cosmos bipinnatus* and the two plants have contrasting leaf and flower shapes. Cultivars in the Flamingo Series of *C. spicata* grow slender, barley-like spikes in shades of silvery pink and look lovely with short blue fescue grass (*Festuca glauca*) and white bacopa or with pink-flowering lamium.

Requirements:

Full sun; likes heat and recovers if allowed to dry out. Pinching results in shorter flower heads but more of them. Try to buy plants not already in bloom; blooming specimens don't transplant well.

~ Cosmos

C. sulfureus varieties have daisy-shaped flowers in bright golds and reds. *C. bipinnatus* is taller with feathery foliage and comes in pink, rose or white with slightly looser, larger flowers. Both are annuals. *C. atrosanguineus* is a tender, tuberous perennial with maroon flowers that smell faintly of chocolate—honest.

Annual or perennial
Height
24 inches to 4 feet
(30 to 120 cm)
Spread
24 inches (60 cm)

Requirements:

Full sun; drought-tolerant; deadhead regularly. Plants may need discreet staking to keep fragile stems from flopping over the pot's edge.

~ Dahlberg daisy

Thymophylla tenuiloba (sometimes listed as *Dyssodia tenuiloba*)

Masses of yellow, dime-size daisies on plants with wiry stems and pungent, feathery foliage make this an appealing choice for hot-colored planters with cannas, dahlias and nasturtiums. It also looks sweet spilling over the edge of an herb basket filled with curly parsley, lemon thyme and chives.

Annual
Height
12 inches (30 cm)
Spread
12 inches (30 cm)

Requirements:

Sun; drought-tolerant. Stems are brittle; transplant with care.

~ Dahlia

Seed-grown types are usually flat, daisy-type flowers in clear yellow, red, orange, pink, lilac or white. Fancier versions are grown from tubers started indoors and planted out after the last frost (consult a catalog or book on summer bulbs for more complete directions; there are several methods). Blooms can be small and round like ping-pong balls or wide and flat like dinner plates; petals can be quilled, spidery, twisted or shaggy. Most bloom from midsummer through fall, making dahlias especially welcome when spring and summer flowers are past their prime. Blooms come in every color but true blue, but I'm sure hybridizers are working on that.

Tender perennial grown
 from seed or tubers
Height
12 inches to 4 feet
(30 to 120 cm)
Spread
12 to 36 inches
(30 to 90 cm)

Requirements:

Full sun; tolerates heat, but not drought. Feed heavily for big, beautiful blooms. Don't pierce the tuber when staking tall varieties. Earwigs can be troublesome.

~ Daylily   *Hemerocallis* cultivars

Hardy perennial
Height
12 to 36 inches
(30 to 90 cm)
Spread
18 to 24 inches
(45 to 60 cm)

Each flower lasts one day, but plants—especially recent introductions—produce several flower-scapes, each with a dozen buds or more. Plants have long, slender, arching leaves. Although the flowers have a trumpet shape similar to a lily's, don't confuse them with true lilies, found in the *Lilium* genus. Flower colors and combinations are vast—from brick-reds with gold throats to yellows that look dusted with glitter to sherbet shades of melon, lime and raspberry. Flower shapes are almost as diverse: ruffled, spidery, flared, flat and double. Dwarf types work especially well in containers; some even rebloom, such as the ubiquitous 'Stella d'Oro', if summers are long enough. A long, deep, well-insulated planter filled with daylilies blooming from early July to late August in complementary colors makes a beautiful above-ground border for a small condominium garden.

Requirements:

Full sun or afternoon shade. Don't plant crowns too deeply or they may rot. Deadhead daily to remove spent blooms, which look like dried-up bits of crepe paper.

~ Dianthus chinensis

Annual
Height
10 inches (25 cm)
Spread
8 inches (20 cm)

Annual dianthus, sometimes called China pinks, have flat flowers with fringed petals atop stiff stems. Colors are bright pink, red or white; white flowers sometimes have halos of pink or red. Perky China pinks are old-fashioned flowers that bloom all summer. Usually they're sold in mixed colors, but if you can find a few all-white plants, combine them with green-and-white English ivy, white *Salvia greggii* and scads of lilac bacopa in a tall, black urn for a sophisticated look.

Requirements:

Full sun; overcrowding may invite fungal diseases.

~ Diascia

Tender perennial
Height
12 inches (30 cm)
Spread
12 inches (30 cm)

The flowers look a bit like smaller, less-complicated snapdragons, but with spurs on the back, like nasturtiums. Color range is mainly mauves and pinks. Lax stems curl up after spilling over container rims.

Requirements:

Sun to part shade.

～ Fuchsia

Tender perennial
Height
*Upright types, about 12
to 24 inches (30 to 60 cm)*
Spread
*12 inches (30 cm)
Trailing types can reach
24 to 36 inches
(60 to 90 cm)*

Lady's eardrops, a common name for fuchsia when ladies wore earrings as well as white gloves and hats, is an apt description of the plant's flowers. Dangling flared-back petals (actually sepals) encircle a protruding tube (a corolla), and prominent pistil and stamens peek out from the bottom. Some flowers are large and plump, while others are narrow and slim. All attract hummingbirds. Colors are red, white, salmon, coral, purple or pink, and often the sepals and corolla are different colors. One of the most versatile fuchsias is 'Gartenmeister Bonstedt', which has loads of slim orange flowers and dark purplish-green leaves on bushy plants. It looks smashing with black sweet potato vine (*Ipomoea batatus* 'Blackie'), lime and nearly-black coleus and purple fountain grass (*Pennisetum setaceum* 'Rubrum').

Requirements:

Part sun to shade; 'Gartenmeister Bonstedt' tolerates more sun than other varieties. Most prefer cool summers, but some new cultivars are more heat-tolerant. Don't allow plants to dry out completely; they prefer consistently moist soil. Although the spent flowers drop off on their own, you'll need to snap off the seedpods that remain to keep the plants blooming.

～ Gazania ringens

Perennial grown as
 annual
Height
8 inches (20 cm)
Spread
10 inches (25 cm)

Solid or bicolor two-inch (5-cm) daisies in red, yellow, white or bronze with gray-green felty leaves. Blooms close on cloudy days and at night. Portulaca have similar characteristics and make good companions; a more subtle partnering is gazania and lotus vine.

Requirements:

Full sun; tolerates drought. Good for dry, windy sites.

~ Geranium   *Pelargonium* spp. and cvs.

Tender perennial
Height
12 to 24 inches
(30 to 60 cm)
Spread
12 to 18 inches
(30 to 45 cm)

For many gardeners, container plants and geraniums are synonymous. Geraniums bloom continuously and their spheres of white, salmon, pink, red and vivid coral florets can readily be seen from a distance. Aged terra-cotta pots, each sporting one scarlet geranium, marching up the steps of a townhouse, never fails to look charming and European, no matter how many times I've seen it.

Requirements:

Sun and heat, and plenty of it. Deadhead when more than half the florets in a flowerhead are spent. If plants get leggy and straggly, pinch off growing tips. Most gardeners treat geraniums like annuals, but you can hold them over winter and replant them next year. Methods for overwintering abound. Here are three:

1. Take stem cuttings a few weeks before the first expected fall frost and root in soilless mix; when rooted, plant in small pots and grow on a sunny windowsill.
2. Leave plants in containers, but cut back by two-thirds and grow indoors in full sun; in late spring, cut back the leggy growth, fertilize and move back outdoors when the weather permits.
3. Store plants bare root (without soil) in a cool, dark spot (a cold cellar is ideal), or store plants in barely moist peat moss to keep them from dehydrating. Replant them in early spring, water and grow indoors until weather permits moving them outdoors again. Don't fertilize until new growth appears. (I've never had great success with this method, but some gardeners swear by it. A damp basement without forced-air heat would help, I suppose.)

Other Types of Geraniums

Ivy geraniums tolerate more shade than common geraniums; leaves are bright, glossy green and flowers come in a wide range of colors.

Balcons geraniums also trail, but they like more sun; colors are limited to salmon or pink. Ivy and balcons geraniums are more difficult to overwinter.

Regal or Martha Washington geraniums (*P. domesticum*) have blooms like azaleas and are usually sold in late winter and early spring. They require cool temperatures at night to continue blooming and are usually spent by the time summer arrives.

Some geraniums are grown for their highly decorative foliage—leaves edged in red and cream or in shapes that are tiny or pointed. For example,

'Vancouver Centennial', a stellar type with star-shaped leaves, has orange-red flowers and lime-green leaves banded with terra cotta—definitely distinctive.

Scented geraniums have fragrant foliage—rose, apricot, cinnamon, lemon or eucalyptus, for example.

～ Gerbera jamesonii

Perennial grown
  as annual
Height
12 inches (30 cm)
Spread
12 inches (30 cm)

Large daisies—often six inches (15 cm) across—on long, sturdy stems. Their yellow centers are sometimes surrounded by cream, pink, orange, yellow or red rays. Blooms mainly in summer and fall; leaves form a rosette at the base of the plant.

Requirements:

Sun or afternoon shade. Take care not to bury the crown when transplanting.

～ Heliotrope *Heliotropium arborescens*

Perennial grown
  as annual
Height
*12 to 18 inches
(30 to 45 cm)*
Spread
*12 to 18 inches
(30 to 45 cm)*

Flat clusters of rich purple flowers on plants with lovely dark green, thick crinkled leaves. Another common name is cherry pie plant in honor of its vanilla/cherry fragrance. 'Marine' is a compact variety, but not as fragrant as 'Fragrant Delight'. Heliotrope looks best planted on its own so both the flowers and foliage can be admired. There are white varieties, but the flowers look slightly tatty when they begin to fade.

Requirements:

Sun to part shade; tolerates heat and humidity, but not drought. Heliotrope pouts if subjected to cool spring temperatures; wait until weather warms up before planting. Deadhead regularly.

～ Impatiens

Perennial grown
  as annual
Height
*6 to 24 inches
(15 to 60 cm)*
Spread
up to 24 inches (60 cm)

It's doubtful anyone—even those who have gardened for only a few months—hasn't encountered impatiens. Although garden selections of wild impatiens weren't introduced until the 1960s, they are a mainstay in today's shady containers. Impatiens suffer the fate of other easy-to-grow plants—they're often shunned because they're so easygoing and ever-present. Yet, it's hard to find a more accommodating plant for shade in such a range of colors. The simple white, lilac and pale pink flowers blend easily in mixed plantings and quickly fill out a container or basket. In Britain, the common name for these plants is busy Lizzies—how apt.

New Guinea hybrids (sometimes called sunshine impatiens) tolerate much more sun, and are more rigid in form than regular impatiens. Flowers are larger and come in vivid pink, red, purple and white. Leaves are longer and darker green. These, and the double-flowered types, which look like miniature roses, are grown from cuttings. Some of the newest impatiens are in the Seashell series, so named because the flowers look like shells (not as flat as regular impatiens). The series also offers a breakthrough in colors: yellow, apricot and pale orange.

Requirements:

I. wallerana prefers shade, although it's common to see half-barrels of healthy impatiens in full sun on city streets and in parks. The large, wooden containers keep roots cool, and the plants get consistent water and fertilizer by parks department staff, which helps mitigate the sunny sites. Don't let the plants dry out completely, although overwatering causes small, sickly yellow leaves. Hot sun causes plants to wilt, and cooler temperatures at night revive the plants; don't mistake wilting for a need for more water. Plants turn mushy at the first hint of frost. New Guinea hybrids need full to part sun and constant moisture.

～ Kingfisher or blue daisy

Felicia amelloides, sometimes *F. bergeriana*

Half-hardy annual
Height
12 inches (30 cm)
Spread
12 inches (30 cm)

Small, blue, yellow-centered daisies with needle-shaped foliage that's almost succulent. Recently available is a variegated variety with white-edged leaves; there's also one with white flowers. Kingfisher daisies suit moss baskets—the plants hug the sides and the flowering stems turn upward.

Requirements:

Sun to part shade. Deadhead regularly.

～ Marguerite daisy

Argyranthemum cultivars, formerly classified in *Chrysanthemum* genus

Tender perennial
Height
12 to 24 inches
(30 to 60 cm)
Spread
12 to 24 inches
(30 to 60 cm)

Cheery primrose, pink or white daisies bloom from spring until fall. 'Summer Melody' has double pink flowers. They are sometimes trained as standards. White 'Sugar Baby' barely reaches 12 inches (30 cm) and is good in window boxes or hanging baskets. A large pot of yellow marguerites, purple trailing petunias, *Plectranthus madagascariensis*, blue nemesia and white million bells (*Calibrachoa* cultivar) were the centerpiece in a collection of containers planted with yellow, white, blue and purple flowers clustered around our patio door one summer. Marguerites are sometimes referred to as Paris daisies.

Requirements:

Sun to part shade.

～ Marigold   *Tagetes* spp. and cvs.

Annual
Height
6 to 24 inches
(15 to 60 cm)
Spread
8 to 18 inches
(20 to 45 cm)

Easygoing marigolds need no introduction, but they could probably do with some better PR. Because they're so widely grown, we've tired of seeing them paired with the equally ubiquitous blue ageratums, red geraniums and white sweet alyssum. Admittedly, the strong colors of single- or double-blooming marigolds can be tough to work with, but thankfully we're becoming less fearful of bright orange, red and gold and using them in more original ways. Mahogany 'Durango Red' with purple heliotrope, bronze ajuga and asparagus fern make a floral Persian carpet. 'Vanilla' is a creamy white, a difficult color to find in annuals. (Unfortunately, the flowers look like dirty socks when they fade.) Various sizes of terra-cotta pots, each filled with a single type of marigold, clustered together on a front porch, offer a simple, cheery look. Fern-leaf marigolds (*T. tenuifolia* 'Lemon Gem', Tangerine Gem' and 'Paprika') are daintier flowers; one or two plants in a window box spill attractively over the edge. Some claim the lacy leaves have a lemony fragrance, but I find they have the same pungency as other marigolds.

Requirements:

Full sun, tolerates drought. Deadhead frequently (*T. tenuifolia* excepted).

~ Nemesia

Annuals and tender
  perennials
Height
12 to 18 inches
(30 to 45 cm)
Spread
10 inches (25 cm)

Annual *N. strumosa* is an intricate flower: petals shaped like two lips—white, pink, yellow, purple or blue—often with a yellow or white "beard" at their base (picture a cross between diascia and scaevola). The flowers grow in clusters at the tips of lax stems. Recently, larger-flowering tender perennial hybrids have come on the market, mainly in white or blue. Perfect in hanging baskets and window boxes. Some are touted as fragrant.

Requirements:

Sun to part shade.

~ Nicotiana

Annuals and perennials
  grown as annuals
Height
12 to 36 inches
(30 to 90 cm)
Spread
12 to 24 inches
(30 to 60 cm)

Nicotiana has tubular flowers that flare out into a star shape. The 12-inch (30-cm) tall Domino and Nikki Series flower in shades of pink, rose, salmon and red, as well as white. *N.* 'Lime Green' is a bit lurid on its own; it's easier on my eyes when it's next to royal purple petunias, heliotrope or mealycup sage. The taller species—*N. alata* and *N. langsdorffii*—are fragrant and send out long-throated, greenish-white flowers. All nicotiana plants have large rosettes of spoon-shaped, basal leaves, which make them difficult to use in mixed planters. Site them in large-diameter pots where their leaves won't crowd out other plants.

Requirements:

Full sun or part shade; heat-tolerant. When deadheading, remove entire flower stalk. Species open at dusk and in evening. Some cultivars stay open in the day, more reliably so if positioned in partial shade.

~ Pansy, Viola   *Viola × wittrockiana, V. cornuta*

Perennials, usually
  grown as annuals
Height
12 inches (30 cm)
Spread
12 inches (30 cm)

Pansies start out as compact plants and grow straggly in the heat of June and July. But who can resist their cute faces? The color and pattern combinations are almost endless. Use by themselves or pair them with just about any plant. Many are sweetly fragrant, too. 'Antique Shades' come in colors of faded chintz. Fragrant, ruffly 'Chalons' and 'Contessa' are blends of royal purple, burgundy and cream, often edged with gold. Violas have slightly smaller blooms, usually in solid colors, including nearly black and clear apricot.

Requirements:

Pansies like cool weather, making them especially suited to spring and fall displays, although some newer hybrids withstand hot summers. They prefer some shade, but tolerate full sun if given adequate water. Frequent deadheading promotes more blooms. Pansies and violas often self-seed. New to the market are Icicle pansies, which bloom spring, summer and fall in my flower border; I've not tried them in containers.

～ Petunia

Perennial grown
 as annual
Height
12 inches (30 cm)
Spread
12 inches (30 cm)
Trailing types
up to 36 inches (90 cm)

Love 'em or hate 'em—few other annuals elicit so much opinion. Most agree, however, that breeders have spent a great deal of attention on the petunia. Up until a few decades ago, most petunias were straggly plants with rose, red, pink, purple or white flowers easily tattered by wind and rain. But they grew like crazy in containers, and people loved them. Soon breeders tempted us with fluffy, double versions, flowers with star patterns and picotee edges, new blue and yellow varieties, cascading plants with long stems, and plants with bigger, smaller or sturdier blooms.

As is so often the case when there's too much of a good thing, gardeners began to tire of petunias—they were everywhere!—and turned to other annuals for easy color. Although older varieties are sweetly fragrant, most look spent by August. The sticky blossoms are a magnet for aphids, and plants need daily deadheading and a severe cutting back in midsummer.

As you might guess, I'm not a fan of petunias; however, there are a few selections worth recommending: anything in the Madness series, especially the silvery pink 'Summer Madness', is a good performer, and the small-flowered Fantasy and Celebrity series look perky most of the summer (the flowers seem to have a bit of starch to them—they're not all droopy and saggy like other varieties). The cool blue of 'Blue Daddy' is lovely in mixed plantings with other old-fashioned flowers such as purple and white browallia, pink impatiens, lobelia or white tuberous begonias.

Hybridizers have continued to tinker with petunias and about eight years ago introduced 'Purple Wave', a flower-laden, well-branched trailer that never needs shearing or deadheading. It was soon followed by Surfinia, Supertunia and Solana Royals petunias, all grown from cuttings, not seed. These bulked-up petunias are ideal in hanging baskets and window boxes (they need diligent feeding to reach their flowering potential). For a subtler look, substitute with cultivars in the *Calibrachoa* genus, which has smaller, daintier, trailing blooms and is closely related to petunias. Often sold under the name million bells, the one-inch (2.5-cm) diameter flat flowers—rose, terra-cotta, yellow, white, purple or pink—have yellow centers. Leaves are small and smooth. One plant fills a six-inch (15-cm) hanging pot; three obliterate the edges of a large container. It's the perfect petunia for non-petunia lovers.

Also worth searching out is *P. integrifolia*, the species from which all these hybrids have come. It has long stems profusely covered with small, deep pink, dark-eyed flowers.

Requirements:

Full or part sun; likes the heat. Fertilize, pinch and deadhead religiously to keep plants blooming. Common petunias fall into two main categories—grandifloras have larger flowers, but can be susceptible to botrytis (a problem in humid climates), and multifloras, which have smaller flowers on smaller plants but are more resistant to botrytis. Shear regular petunias back by two-thirds in midsummer. They'll bounce back with more flowers and compact growth. Million bells seem to be immune to everything, including aphids, and never need deadheading.

∿ Portulaca

Annual
Height
2 to 3 inches (5 to 7 cm)
Spread
12 inches (30 cm)

Small flowers—reminiscent of single roses—on short, shrubby plants with succulent, needle-like leaves. Flowers on newer varieties like the Sundial series tend to stay open on cloudy days. Most portulacas are so short they barely reach the top of a container where they can be noticed. However, they make a colorful mat of blooms under standard plants. Up until recently, cell packs usually contained a kaleidoscope of colors, not always what's wanted when planning a specific color combination. But it's now possible to buy packs of single colors.

Requirements:

Full sun; extremely drought-resistant.

∼ Salvia, Sage *Salvia farinacea*

Perennial grown as
  annual or perennial,
  depending on species
Height
Mealycup sage
(S. farinacea): 24 to 36
inches (60 to 90 cm)
Culinary sage
(S. officinalis): 24 inches
(60 cm)
Salvia (S. splendens):
12 to 24 inches
(30 to 60 cm)
Spread
12 inches (30 cm)

Annual mealycup sage flowers are usually tall, narrow, violet-blue spires, a shape and color not that common to annuals. 'Victoria' is a well-branched royal blue; 'White Porcelain' is dusty white; 'Strata' has blue-and-white spikes. The royal blue mealycup sage works well in various color schemes. Combine it with deep pink fuchsia, lilac-blue petunias and silver helichrysum in a large wicker basket to create a soft, romantic look. For a fresh, crisp vignette, try it with pale yellow marguerite daisies, a small blue-leaved hosta, white million bells, blue nemesia and variegated *Plectranthus madagascariensis* 'Miller's Wife'.

Grown for its pebbly gray-green leaves, culinary sage (*s. officinalis*), a hardy perennial, sends out a few lilac flowers in summer. Variegated sages—the white, purple and green 'Tricolor' and green and yellow 'Icterina'—are less hardy. 'Purpurea', with purple and dark green leaves, is beautiful partnered with clear pink flowers such as miniature roses or portulaca.

Varieties of annual salvia (*S. splendens*) are easily recognized: the stop-sign red types are most common, but there are more subtle shades available: greenish-white, dusky salmon and rich purple. To mitigate the rigid, stiff flower spikes, pair salvias with soft, mounding flowers or arching, swaying grasses. Hummingbirds love annual salvia. Related to *S. splendens*, but with more graceful, natural-looking blooms, is *S. coccinea*, commonly called scarlet sage. 'Lady in Red' is a clear, true red; flowers from early summer to fall.

Growers bring different salvia species and cultivars onto the market each year, and it's worth picking up a cell pack or two to experiment. I'm currently enamoured with white *S. greggii*—it has the constitution of *S. splendens* and the grace of *S. coccinea*.

Requirements:

Full sun; heat-tolerant. Pinch mealycup sage plants when young to make them bushier. *S. splendens* needs consistent watering.

∼ Snapdragon *Antirrhinum majus*

Perennial grown
  as annual
Height
6 to 36 inches
(15 to 90 cm)
Spread
8 to 12 inches
(20 to 30 cm)

Old-fashioned flowers in a range of colors from jewel tones to soft pastels. The blooms, arranged vertically along each stem, look more like butterflies than dragons, which are much nicer creatures to have in your garden. Dwarf varieties are usually available in mixed colors; taller types are sold by single color, making them easier to use in color-coordinated displays. Tall varieties make good focal points in a large container. Floriferous trailing snapdragons are becoming more readily available.

The Potted Garden

Requirements:

Full or part sun. Grows well in cool temperatures and is tolerant of light frosts. Cut back after first flush of bloom to promote another set of flowers. Plants often flag near the end of a hot summer.

~ Swan River daisy   *Brachyscome iberidifolia*

Annual
Height
10 to 20 inches
(25 to 50 cm)
Spread
10 to 20 inches
(25 to 50 cm)

Perky lavender-blue or white mounds of daisies on bushy plants with ferny foliage. I don't think there's ever been a year when I haven't included these blue daisies in a few containers. There are also several selections in yellow, pink and mauve. I'm not sure why breeders thought it necessary to improve on the original lovely blue. The yellow centers and blue ray florets of Swan River daisies are ideal for experimenting with the theory of color echoes: pair them with soft yellow tuberous begonias or snapdragons and blue nemesia or *Convolvulus sabatius*.

Requirements:

Sun to part shade.

~ Sweet alyssum   *Lobularia maritima*

Half-hardy annual
Height
4 to 6 inches
(10 to 15 cm)
Spread
12 inches (30 cm)

Spreading mats of tiny flowers clustered at the ends of stems clothed in equally small leaves. Sweet alyssum flowers are usually white or rose, but purple, ivory and apricot strains are also available that make a good ground cover under standards or a filler in window boxes and hanging baskets. "Sweet" refers to the plant's honey-like fragrance, which is noticeable when masses of it are planted; bees love it.

Requirements:

Full sun to part shade. Shear back when plants begin to throw out fewer blooms; they grow back quickly.

～ Thread-leaved tickseed *Coreopsis verticillata*

Hardy perennial
Height
12 to 24 inches
(30 to 60 cm)
Spread
12 to 24 inches
(30 to 60 cm)

Of the several species of coreopsis, the thread-leaved variety is especially suited to containers because of its attractive feathery foliage and long period of bloom. Small yellow daisies appear in midsummer for four to six weeks, and seem to dance on the wiry stems. 'Moonbeam' has pale yellow flowers that mix well with icy blues. 'Zagreb' is shorter (about one foot/30 cm) and a darker yellow.

Requirements:

Full sun; heat-tolerant. After most of blooms fade, shear off the top, and you may get a second burst of flowers.

～ Verbena

Perennial grown
 as annual
Height
8 to 12 inches
(20 to 30 cm)
Spread
12 inches (30 cm)
Some trailing types

Star-shaped flowers, usually in deep rose, purple or red with a white eye, packed onto two- to three-inch (5- to 7-cm) wide clusters on erect, bushy plants. Softer in color is the aptly named 'Peaches and Cream'. Verbenas' cheerful good looks and accommodating nature make them suitable companions for many plants. Trailing types include 'Homestead Purple', a reliable bloomer with golf ball–sized blooms, and smaller 'Imagination', also purple. Trailing verbena also comes in red, silvery pink, lavender and white.

Requirements:

Full sun or afternoon shade; heat- and drought-tolerant. Pinch growing tips to promote bushiness; deadhead, too. Plants are susceptible to powdery mildew; the trailing Tapien and Temari series are said to be less so.

～ Zinnia

Annual
Height
Mexican zinnia: Z.
haageana *(sometimes
listed as* Z. angustifolia)
12 inches (30 cm)
Z. elegans *varieties: 12 to
36 inches (30 to 90 cm)*
Spread
12 inches (30 cm)

The white or orange-gold one-inch (2.5-cm) wide daisies of *Z. haageana* (Mexican Zinna) appear nonstop from summer to frost on wiry stems. The common zinnia (*Z. elegans*) has larger flowers in a wide range of colors on stiffer-stemmed plants. Especially trendy is lime-green 'Envy'. Most nurseries sell mixed colors; if you want a specific shade, you may need to grow it from seed, which is easy.

Left: The more ornate the container, the simpler the plant combination can be. Low-growing plants at the base of this imposing cast-iron pedestal won't obscure the details of its design as the season progresses. Even without plants, a massive container like the example shown here could act as a focal point in winter.

Opposite page: The illusion of the classically styled statue watering the double impatiens and purple trailing lobelia planted at her feet creates a charming vignette in a formal garden. On the opposite side of the path is a similarly planted container.

Right: Glossy hosta leaves and the patina on an antique white urn set the stage for a vibrant combination of purple heliotrope and angelonia, orange and yellow Mexican sunflowers (*Tithonia rotundifolia*), and gray helichrysum. Be generous with the number of plants in a container and plant much more closely than what's recommended for traditional garden settings.

Overleaf: Walls and fences are prime spots for container plants. A yellow tuberous begonia and a few white trailing lobelia plants brighten up a somber green wall of Boston ivy.

Right: Various sizes of pots with an ▶ eclectic sampling of plants serve as a mini-flower bed near a front door. The smaller pots can be moved around to create different effects, or whisked away to make room for new combinations. Container gardening provides the perfect opportunity to try new plants and colors on a small scale.

◀ *Left*: Placed separately, these three pretty pots might be easily overlooked. Grouped together, they become an eye-catching composition of pink, purple and lime-green flowers and foliage. From left to right: pink streptocarpus, purple pansies, Persian shield (*Strobilanthes dyerianus*) and 'Limelight' helichrysum. The small terra-cotta strawberry pot of pansies will need watering more frequently than the two glazed containers flanking it.

Requirements:

Z. haageana doesn't grow well in cool springs, but takes off when weather is hot; it's forgiving if you forget to water. Unlike other zinnias, this species is unbothered by mildew. *Z. elegans* also performs well in heat, but don't allow plants to dry out completely. Most cultivars suffer from mildew, which is exacerbated in closely planted containers. Combine with plants of different heights so air can circulate freely around the zinnias' leaves.

Trailers and Climbers

Vines are wonderful, versatile container plants. When trained to climb and clamber over obelisks, bamboo teepees or decorative wire supports, they quickly fill the vertical growing space in a container garden without requiring much room at ground level—perfect solutions for small gardens. Quick-growing annual vines like morning glories and sweetpeas can create a green privacy screen in a few weeks. When allowed to trail, vines soften the harsh edges of containers, camouflage the sides of less attractive pots, weave their magic through the feet of other, more upright plants, and knit together to form glorious spheres of foliage and flowers in hanging moss baskets. Also included in this category are trailing plants that aren't necessarily true vines, but plants with long, lax stems that have an easygoing, relaxed air. It's the rare container that doesn't benefit from the addition of a well-chosen vine or trailing plant. What would window boxes and hanging baskets be without them?

∼ Australian fan-flower   *Scaevola aemula*

Perennial grown
 as annual
Spread
18 inches (45 cm)

Ten years ago, few in North America had seen Australian fan-flower, but it's everywhere these days. The purplish-blue, one-inch (2.5-cm) flowers look like tiny daisies cut in half and appear all summer long without flagging. Toothed leaves are spoon-shaped.

Requirements:

Full sun to part shade. Although extremely heat-tolerant, plants are fussy about moisture. Never let them dry out completely, but don't let soil remain soggy.

～ Bacopa also listed as *Sutera cordata*

Perennial grown
 as annual
Spread
*12 to 24 inches
(30 to 60 cm)*

Bacopa took containers by storm a few years ago, and many of its cultivars are appropriately named: 'Snowflake', 'Snow Falls' and 'Snowstorm'. Plants are covered with tiny, five-petaled flowers that cascade in a white sheet over the edge of containers. 'Mauve Mist' is a rather insipid lavender; 'Penny Candy Rose' is a much livelier color.

Requirements:

Sun to part shade. Plants are slow to recover if allowed to dry out. On extremely hot days, move them to cool shade.

～ Bidens ferulifolia

Tender perennial
Spread
*24 to 36 inches
(60 to 90 cm)*

Bright gold, five-petaled daisies bob along on thick mats of ferny leaves and wiry stems. Not for neat freaks, 'Golden Goddess' (an enticing cultivar name) has a wild, sprawling habit that quickly fills a hanging basket or window box. 'Goldie' is less rambunctious. Seed-grown plants are more upright; most nurseries sell plants grown from cuttings, which grow more prostrate. Bidens blooms from the time you plant it until frost.

Requirements:

Sun to part shade. Dislikes soggy soil. Deadheading isn't necessary to keep bidens in bloom, but trimming out the dead flowers (if you have the time and patience) does improve its appearance.

～ Black-eyed Susan vine   *Thunbergia alata*

Perennial grown
 as annual
Height
3 to 8 feet (90 to 240 cm)

Flat, five-petaled buff or orange-yellow flowers. Most have a purplish-brown eye, but you can sometimes find plants without the dark centers. Twining vines grow up trellises or cascade down the sides of a hanging basket. My favorite way to grow them is to place an upside-down tomato cage in a large pot, tie the bottom prongs of the wire cage into a peak and let six or so vines climb to the top. It makes an interesting pyramid of flowers.

Requirements:

Full or part sun; likes warmth and humidity. Don't let plants dry out.

⌒ Clematis

Hardy perennial
Height
3 to 10 feet
(90 to 300 cm)

Hybrids have large, usually flat flowers (actually sepals that surround the small petals in the center). Species often feature smaller, nodding, urn-shaped blooms. Seedheads are swirling, fluffy novelties. The vines attach themselves easily to wire or string by means of short leaf stems; you'll need to tie stems to bulkier supports. Shorter varieties meander through plants in a large container and spill over the edge. Or train one up an elegant obelisk. Cultivars of *C. alpina* and *viticella* are the hardiest.

Requirements:

Full or part sun. Clematis likes a bit of shade at its roots, and the rim of the pot it's planted in may provide enough, but another option is to use smaller containers with shorter plants near it. Containers need to be at least 18 inches (45 cm) deep. Plant a clematis about two inches (5 cm) deeper than it was growing in its pot to trigger the growth of new stems. Provide support immediately because stems are brittle and easily whipped around in wind. They're also impossible to untangle once they start scrambling over each other. You'll likely want to overwinter a clematis, so choose an appropriate container and move it to a sheltered spot when frost hits. Most clematis need pruning, and timing depends on when it blooms. Those that bloom on new wood (late-blooming varieties) are cut back to 10 inches (25 cm) in very early spring just before leaves begin to bud. Those that bloom in spring or in summer are generally pruned after blooming. Consult a perennial book or one devoted to clematis for more precise pruning instructions for particular varieties.

⌒ Convolvulus sabatius

Tender perennial
Spread
24 inches (60 cm)

This popular basket plant looks like a miniature version of 'Heavenly Blue' morning glory. Trailing stems have silvery bluish-green oval leaves and are covered with blooms the size of a quarter The flowers stay open longer than morning glories, but do close at night and on cloudy days.

Requirements:

Full sun to part shade; drought-resistant.

～ Lantana camara

Tender perennial
Spread
24 to 36 inches
(60 to 90 cm)

Round clusters of white, pink, red, orange or yellow flowers on sturdy stems with crinkled leaves that are happy arching over the edges of a pot (blooms look similar to those on trailing verbena). Or tie stems to a thin bamboo pole to create a mop-topped standard. The flowers on some yellow varieties turn pink as they age, giving flowerheads a two-tone effect. One especially vibrant cultivar is 'Gold Mound', with deep gold blooms and bright green crinkled leaves edged with a wide band of yellow-green.

Requirements:

Full sun; likes the heat, but will tolerate cooler weather in late summer. Pinch for more branches.

～ Lobelia erinus

Perennial grown
  as annual
Height
Trailing types reach about
18 inches (45 cm),
compact edging types
grow to about 6 inches
(15 cm)

Scads of dainty blue, rose, lavender or white flowers. The upright, bushy clumps of edging lobelia bloom most of the summer, but they aren't as graceful in containers as their blowsy cousins, the trailing varieties. (Read plant labels carefully to make sure you're getting the type you want; they look similar when young.) 'Cambridge Blue' is a cornflower blue, 'Sapphire Blue' is a rich blue with white centers—both are trailing types. 'Lilac Fountain' and 'White Fountain' are two more aptly named trailing types. *L. ricardii*, grown from cuttings, is less likely to brown out during hot summers as long as plants aren't allowed to dry out. Double-flowering blue 'Kathleen Mallard' is commonly available.

Requirements:

Full sun to part shade for clumping types; part shade for trailing varieties. Unfortunately, the trailing types often turn crisp in summer heat. If well established before heat strikes, plants usually hold up. Afternoon shade and regular watering help, too. Shear plants back partway when they get ratty, but don't whack off all the stems at one length; stagger the stem lengths so the haircut doesn't look so severe. Plants rebloom quickly.

∼ Mandevilla x amabilis

Tender perennial
Height
*5 to 6 feet
(150 to 180 cm)*

Big, trumpet-shaped flowers—sometimes four inches (10 cm) across— with a tropical look and glossy, thick, dark green oval leaves on twining vines. Pink 'Alice du Pont' is readily available, but more varieties have recently come on the market, including a pure white. Plants bloom from early summer until frost. Mandevilla, like passionflower, is a rampant vine best left planted singly in large containers.

Requirements:

Full sun or afternoon shade; likes heat. Use a soil-based planting mix in a large pot, and pinch stem tips to encourage branching.

∼ Morning glory *Ipomoea tricolor*

Annual
Height
up to 12 feet (400 cm)

No flower is more true blue than 'Heavenly Blue' morning glory. Equally lovely are the lavender, rose, burgundy and tie-dyed varieties. The twining vines have large, funnel-shaped blooms that unfurl in the morning and close up in the afternoon. Plants grow quickly—provide a sturdy teepee of bamboo stakes or an obelisk for them to climb or they'll quickly become a matted mess. They're good for a screen on a porch or balcony.

Requirements:

Full sun and lots of heat. Don't overfertilize or there will be more leaves and fewer flowers. Start seeds directly in container after danger of frost has passed or transplant purchased seedlings without disturbing roots.

∼ Nasturtium *Tropaeolum majus*

Annual
Spread
24 inches (60 cm) or more
Bushy, dwarf varieties also available

Bright, edible funnel-shaped nasturtiums have a peppery fragrance and flavor. Flowers, which sometimes sport a little spur in back, can be yellow, red, mahogany, orange or a cream-and-pale red bicolor, called 'Peach Melba'. Nasturtium foliage is ornamental too, reminiscent of small lily pads. 'Alaska' has white blotches on its leaves and 'Empress of India' has rich, velvety scarlet flowers and nearly blue leaves.

Requirements:

Full or part sun. Too much fertilizer results in lots of leaves but few flowers. Although plants relish the heat, roots like to be kept cool and have plenty of room to roam, which explains why plants often fail to thrive in small plastic hanging baskets and window boxes. Transplant purchased seedlings with minimal root disturbance. They're a favorite of aphids.

~ Passionflower *Passiflora caerulea*

Tender perennial
Height
10 feet (300 cm)

It would be difficult to find a more intricately designed flower—or a more vigorous perennial vine. Fragrant, five-inch (12-cm) wide purple, white or pale yellow flowers grow on plants with large, three-lobed leaves. It climbs via tendrils. The common purple variety has white petals and a fringe of purple in the middle. The whole confection is finally topped with a complex arrangement of pistil and stamens. The blooms look a bit like flowery wheels.

Requirements:

Full sun, soil-based mix and large pot. Add vermiculite or perlite to improve drainage. Don't let plants dry out, but beware of soggy soils or they may rot. Misting with water encourages buds to form.

~ Potato vine *Solanum* spp. and cvs.

Tender perennial
Height
about 6 feet (180 cm)

White potato vine (*S. jasminoides* 'Album') has slender, pointed leaves and starry, white, fragrant flowers. A variegated version has leaves with gold edges. Shrubby blue potato bush (*S. rantonnetii*) doesn't twine, and is often trained as a standard. Its flowers are clear, periwinkle blue. Both species have prominent yellow stamens; yellow-flowering companions make a pleasing color echo.

Requirements:

Full sun; likes the heat.

~ Purple bell vine *Rhodochiton atrosanguineus*

Perennial grown
 as annual
Height
8 feet (240 cm)

Intriguing dark purple-and-red bells, about two inches (5 cm) long, dangle from vines that climb via twisting leaf stems. The leaves are heart-shaped.

Requirements:

One of the more shade-tolerant flowering vines, although purple bell vine reaches its full potential in full sun. It requires a long, warm growing season to bloom, so the vine may not put on much of a show until late summer.

～ Sweetpea *Lathyrus odoratus*

Annual
Height
6 feet (180 cm)

Vining types of sweetpeas have a wider color range than the compact, bushy forms, although compact sweetpeas make good container plants, too. Wavy, sometimes ruffled, flowers in red, blue, lavender, pink and every shade in between are borne on sturdy stems; the vines, which climb via tendrils, sport blue-green leaves. Not all cultivars are fragrant, but most of the old-fashioned, smaller-flowering varieties are. 'Cupani', a vivid purple and burgundy bicolor, smells like grape jelly.

Requirements:

Full sun and cool weather; where summers are hot, provide sweetpeas with afternoon shade. They can be seeded directly in pots, a good option because plants dislike having their roots disturbed. Pick flowers as they fade or the plants will stop blooming entirely.

～ Sweet potato vine *Ipomoea batatus*

Tender perennial
Spread
36 inches (90 cm)

The shape of the deeply lobed leaves is interesting, but the colors—deep burgundy black 'Blackie' and the lively chartreuse 'Marguerita'—are the real draw. Newer selections have pink, green and white leaves or light green leaves with black veins. 'Marguerita' is a natural with boldly colored coleus and coral fuchsia. 'Blackie' is the perfect foil for hot pink verbena and fuzzy silver sage (*Salvia argentea*). When you empty your containers in the fall, look for the little tubers that form undergound—the plant comes by its common name honestly.

Requirements:

Sun or part shade. Don't rush the season; plants dislike cool nights and put on new growth only when summer heats up.

Foliage Foils

Flowering plants look even more beautiful when displayed against trailing or upright forms of foliage plants. In fact, a large container planted with contrasting leaf shapes, textures and colors—and no flowers—can be every bit as riveting as one filled with colorful blossoms. Several of the plants in the following list are perennial herbs with lovely flowers as well as ornamental foliage. I've included them because they're primarily grown for their beautiful leaves, which last longer than their blooms.

⁓ Ajuga reptans

Hardy perennial
Height
4 to 8 inches
(10 to 20 cm)
Spread
10 inches (25 cm) or more

A hardy ground cover that spreads by runners. Depending on the variety, the smooth, five-inch (12-cm) long oval leaves can be shiny green, have a purple cast, or be variegated with cream or pink. 'Burgundy Glow' has green, pink and cream leaves. 'Metallica Crispa' has puckered leaves with a metallic sheen. Grown mainly for their foliage, the plants do have pretty purple-blue or white flower spikes in early summer.

Requirements:

Sun to full shade.

⁓ Artemisia

Hardy perennial
Height
24 to 36 inches
(60 to 90 cm)
Spread
24 to 36 inches
(60 to 90 cm)

Artemisias are silver-leaved plants, most with lacy or filigreed aromatic foliage. The yellow flowers are inconspicuous. 'Powis Castle' and 'Valerie Finnis' have a particularly attractive sheen to their leaves. They're a perfect foil for large-leaved plants, such as sun-tolerant hosta cultivars, bergenias or cannas.

Requirements:

Full sun. If holding over winter, cut back hard in the spring to force new growth. Taller varieties may flop; stake as needed or cut them back to prompt compact new growth.

∼ Bergenia cordifolia

Hardy perennial
Height
*12 to 18 inches
(30 to 45 cm)*
Spread
*12 to 18 inches
(30 to 45 cm)*

Thick, cabbage-like leaves—glossy green on top, greenish-burgundy underneath—form large clumps. Cooler temperatures intensify the burgundy color. Flower clusters—a somewhat lurid pink, sometimes white—rise above the leaves in early spring. The delicate foliage of astilbe makes a pleasing contrast in an all-perennial container.

Requirements:

Part shade; does best in large pots.

∼ Coleus   *Solenostemon scutellarioides*

Tender perennial
Height
*12 to 24 inches
(30 to 60 cm)*
Spread
*12 to 24 inches
(30 to 60 cm)*

Breeders certainly have been busy with coleus in the past few years—it's the foliage plant of the millennium. Once highly prized by our grandmothers' generation, coleus fell out of favor, along with cannas and castor bean plants, two other favorites of the '30s and '40s that are also back in our gardens. Coleus leaves can be narrow and pointed, lobed like an oak leaf, or crinkly and fringed. The range in color variegations is even wider: pink, cream, chartreuse, near-black, burgundy, red, orange and salmon. All produce the same spikes of wishy-washy, lavender flowers that are best removed so as not to detract from the gorgeous foliage. A massive container with different types of coleus looks like a leafy rendering of rubies and emeralds. Try highlighting a flower color with a matching coleus, such as white wax begonias with a lime-yellow and white coleus, or black and burgundy coleus with black and burgundy pansies.

Requirements:

Part sun; tolerates heat and is sensitive to frosts. Pinch branch tips and remove flowerheads as they form for bushier plants. Prefers a nitrogen-based fertilizer.

∼ Coral bells   *Heuchera* spp. and cvs.

Hardy perennial
Height
*12 to 18 inches
(30 to 45 cm)*
Spread
*12 to 18 inches
(30 to 45 cm)*

Coral bells is grown mainly for its luxurious foliage, but its wands of dainty pink or white flowers are pretty, too. Cultivars may have beautiful lobed or ruffled leaves in a range of shades from silvery green to deepest chocolate–maroon. Some of the newer dark chocolate–colored selections have a heavy, drab look, especially if paired with clear white or pink flowers. A lemony thread-leaved coreopsis or periwinkle blue pansy might be a more sympathetic choice. Or let one dark, dramatic coral bells go solo in an elegant stone planter.

Requirements:

Full sun where summers are cool; part shade where it's hot and humid. Don't let the crown get too wet when watering or it may rot. If overwintering in a container, avoid using too much peat or other acidic amendments; heucheras like slightly alkaline soil.

∼ Golden creeping Jenny   *Lysimachia nummularia* 'Aurea'

Hardy perennial
Height
2 inches (5 cm)
Spread
far-reaching

A container is likely the only place you'll want to grow golden creeping Jenny—she doesn't creep, she gallops. The yellow-leaved 'Aurea' is more attractive—and slightly less rambunctious—than the green-leaved species. Round, gold leaves are spaced closely together—almost overlapping—on wiry stems. Bright yellow flowers, nearly the same size as the leaves, briefly appear in early summer. Let stems trail over the edges of a hanging basket or carpet the base of a standard rose.

Requirements:

Part sun to shade. Almost indestructible, but the plants look best when moisture is constant.

∼ Dusty miller   *Senecio cineraria*

Perennial grown
 as annual
Height
*8 to 12 inches
(20 to 30 cm)*
Spread
*12 to 18 inches
(30 to 45 cm)*

Until gardeners started experimenting with different gray-leaved herbs and perennials, dusty miller was about the only touch of gray found in containers. Equally at home with soft blue or lilac flowers or brazen hot oranges and reds, dusty miller is a peace maker, albeit an often overused one. Licorice plant, lotus vine, sage and lamium have more interesting forms and texture.

Requirements:

Full or part sun.

∼ Echeveria

Tender perennial
Height
about 6 inches (15 cm)
Spread
about 6 inches (15 cm)

Similar in appearance to hens and chicks (*Sempervivum tectorum*), but leaves and rosettes are larger, more glaucous, sculptural and fleshy. Even small plants are relatively expensive, but they can be used as a focal point for a grouping of pots. (Incidentally, it's the plant shown on the cover.)

Requirements:

Full sun; free-draining, gritty soil.

∼ English ivy *Hedera helix*

Hardy and tender
   perennials
Spread
*12 inches to 5 feet
(30 to 150 cm)*

Non-gardeners and gardeners alike know English ivy with its dark green, three-pointed leaves. However, it's worth searching out the variegated varieties, especially the green-and-yellow marbled ones, or those with curly or sharply dissected leaves. Although ivy is extremely common in containers, it always looks fresh and elegant. Plants grow quickly, but not aggressively so, and mask the edges of containers and planters with graceful green skirts that highlight the other plants in the mix. Its pliable stems are easy to train on wire topiary forms.

Requirements:

Sun or shade; tolerates summer's heat, but it can be grown in spring containers, too. Plants need consistent moisture and are extremely easy to overwinter indoors.

∼ Ferns

Hardy perennials
Height
*12 inches to 4 feet
(30 to 120 cm)*
Spread
about 18 inches (45 cm)

Many ferns make superb container plants, ranging from tall fronds of familiar ostrich fern (*Matteuccia struthiopteris*) to the more prostrate form of squirrel's-foot fern (*Davallia trichomanoides*), effective in moss-lined hanging baskets. Christmas fern (*Polystichum acrostichoides*) is a well-rounded fern: it has a classic profile with glossy green evergreen fronds about two feet (60 cm) tall. Not all ferns are green: a simple black urn filled with the green, burgundy and silver triangular fronds of Japanese painted ferns (*Athyrium niponicum* 'Pictum') makes an elegant statement.

Requirements:

Shade and moist soil.

∼ Hens and chicks   *Sempervivum tectorum*

Hardy perennial
Height
rosettes of leaves, 3 inches
(7 cm)
flower stalks, 12 inches
(30 cm)
Spread
12 to 18 inches
(30 to 45 cm)

Two- to three-inch (5- to 7- cm) rosettes of succulent leaves (the hens) surrounded by smaller rosettes (the chicks) sit snugly together along the soil's surface. In late summer, the large rosettes send out tall, scaly stems topped with reddish flowers—a space-age look. Rosettes can be green, maroon, a combination of the two or covered with cobweb-like hairs. Mix several varieties in a wide, shallow container or trough for a patchwork effect.

Requirements:

Full sun; gritty soil. Water and feed sparingly.

∼ Hosta

Hardy perennial
Height
6 to 36 inches
(15 to 90 cm)
Spread
Plants are usually wider
than their height.

Sometimes called the ultimate foliage plants, hostas do seem to come in a color, shape and size to suit any circumstance. From the glaucous, puckered, spoon-shaped leaves of *H. sieboldiana* 'Elegans' to the dainty, lance-shaped 'Lemon Lime' or variegated *H. venusta* 'Variegata', there's a hosta to meet every request. And if there isn't, breeders will have it for us next year. There may already be hundreds to choose from, but dozens of new ones appear every spring, some with differences only an aficionado could detect. All hostas are amenable to life in a container; however the truly massive types need an equally massive pot. Plants overwinter easily.

Large cultivars can go solo in a pot while small varieties are good as accents at the edge of containers filled with various flowering plants. The scapes of hostas' small lily-like flowers that appear in summer shouldn't be discounted, either. They're usually lilac or white, some very fragrant, such as those on white-flowering *H. plantaginea*, sometimes called August lily, or the larger-flowering cultivar 'Grandiflora' or 'Royal Standard'. 'Krossa Regal' is an upright, vase-shaped specimen that can be underplanted.

Requirements:

Full shade to part sun with consistently moist soil. If you're overwintering hostas in containers, repotting may be necessary after a year or two: hostas are lusty growers. If slugs are a problem, choose thick-leaved, puckered varieties, which are less desirable to snack on.

〜 Lamium

Hardy perennial
Height
6 inches (15 cm)
Spread
up to 36 inches (90 cm)

When planting lamium with other plants, make sure they can stand up to its rambunctious tendencies. However, lamium is lovely enough to go it alone with its heart-shaped silver leaves edged with green on trailing stems. 'Beacon Silver' has clusters of small tubular pink flowers; 'White Nancy' has white blooms. 'Golden Anniversary' has green leaves edged with a thick band of bright chartreuse and a silver stripe in the center and lilac flowers.

Requirements:

Grows more vigorously in sun, but tolerates shade. Prefers constant moisture. Shear in midsummer if it's too lanky.

〜 Licorice plant   *Helichrysum petiolare*

Tender perennial
Spread
*24 to 26 inches
(60 to 90 cm)*

When I first became interested in container gardening years ago, about the only books available on the subject were published in Britain. Many of the photos featured licorice plant, a dense sprawling plant with small, round, felty silver leaves. I felt my container schemes would be incomplete without this bit of sparkling silver foliage. Calls to large nurseries in Canada produced no results, so I began dialing nurseries in the U.S. that might ship here (this was before the joys of e-commerce and before I fully appreciated the intricacies of shipping plants through Canadian customs). When I was on hold with a nursery in Minnesota for 20 minutes, I knew I had crossed over from being a casual weekend gardener to an obsessive plant junkie.

I still like licorice plant, and these days it's as easy to find as marigolds and petunias. It complements all flower colors from glowing oranges, reds and golds to cool blues, lilacs and pinks. Other helichrysum variations are more recently available, including varieties with variegated green-and-silver leaves, pale gold leaves and plants with small leaves the size of a baby's fingernail. The basic licorice plant grows more vigorously than its variations.

Requirements:

Sun or shade. Prune for bushier, less trailing plants. Although it has fuzzy silver leaves, which usually indicates drought-resistance, don't allow helichrysum to dry out.

Direct Seeding in Pots

Many annuals are easy to grow from seed, and those that bloom a few weeks after sowing are especially good candidates for seeding directly into containers. However, if you live where summers are short, with perhaps 60 to 70 frost-free days each year, direct seeding may not be a practical option. Early fall frosts may strike down your plants soon after they start blooming.

Annuals with root systems that resent transplanting are also good choices for planting *in situ*. However, sometimes it makes more sense to buy young plants which might bloom sooner than those started from seed in a container. Be sure to exercise extra care when transplanting.

Below is a list of annual flowers that grow quickly from seed.

You don't need to devote an entire container to seed-started plants. Try poking in a few nasturtium seeds near the rim of a large pot and enjoy the new look they give the design once they start blooming.

Fast and Easy Annuals
Calendula (*C. officinalis*)

Cosmos (*C. bipinnatus*)

Morning glory (*Ipomoea tricolor*)

Nasturtium (*Tropaeolum majus*)

Portulaca (*P. grandiflora*)

Sweet alyssum (*Lobularia maritima*)

Sweetpea (*Lathyrus odoratus*)

Zinnia (*Z. elegans*)

～ Lotus vine   *L. berthelotti*

Tender perennial
Spread
30 inches (75 cm)

Although listed in the foliage category because of its attractive silvery, feathery leaves, lotus vine could also be included in the category of flowering trailing and spreading plants because it also has bright gold, orange or red flowers. A common name for the plant is parrot's beak, which refers to the flower's shape. However, because lotus vine needs a long season to bloom, its primary use is for foliage contrast.

Requirements:

Full sun to part shade. Plants shed leaves if kept too dry.

～ Ornamental kale, cabbage   *Brassica oleracea*

Annual
Height
12 inches (30 cm)
Spread
*12 to 18 inches
(30 to 45 cm)*

Cool fall days and nights intensify the red, pink, white or green leaves of ornamental kale. Some varieties have lacy, frilly leaves, but most look like colorful cabbages. Five or six small plants set tightly in a container, positioned so the top is slightly domed, looks like a giant, colorful pincushion.

Requirements:

Full or part sun. When temperatures fall below 20°F (–6°C), the plants turn brown and mushy and begin to smell like rotten cabbage.

～ Perilla frutescens crispa

Half-hardy annual
Height
24 to 36 inches
(60 to 90 cm)
Spread
24 to 36 inches
(60 to 90 cm)

Shiny, reddish-purple leaves with ruffled edges. Usually self-seeding isn't an issue for container plants; however, perilla is shameless. I grew two plants on a patio one summer and faced dozens of volunteer seedlings the next spring, sprouting in the cracks between the brick pavers. Fortunately, they were easily uprooted.

Requirements:

Full sun to part shade. Tolerates drought.

～ Persian shield   *Strobilanthes dyeranus*

Tender perennial
Height
36 inches (90 cm)
Spread
36 inches (90 cm)

Not a plant for the timid—the plant's thick, textured leaves are 6 inches (15 cm) long, 2 inches (5 cm) wide, and dark green with an iridescent sheen on top and dark purple underneath. Plants can get quite hefty, quickly filling a half-barrel in a season. Younger plants have better color and aren't as leggy.

Requirements:

Sun or part shade. Intense sun may scorch leaves. Because of its size, this plant is difficult to keep over the winter, but cuttings are easy to root.

～ Pineapple mint   *Mentha suaveolens*

Hardy perennial
Height
12 to 18 inches
(30 to 45 cm)
Spread
18 to 24 inches
(45 to 60 cm)

The prettiest member of the mint family, pineapple mint has bright green, one-inch (2.5-cm) long leaves rimmed with a crisp white edge. Gently rub the leaves to release their minty fragrance.

Requirements:

Sun or shade. Withstands drying out. Shear mid-season to remove less-than-attractive flowers to refresh foliage and to promote branching.

～ Plectranthus madagascariensis

Tender perennial
Spread
36 inches (90 cm)

Variegated cultivars of this relative of Swedish ivy are the prettiest—look for 'Miller's Wife' or 'Variegated Mintleaf', both of which have sturdy, scalloped leaves with irregular white edges. The leaves smell slightly minty when crushed. One plant quickly grows into a thick veil of trailing stems.

Requirements:

Part shade.

~Rosemary *Rosmarinus officinalis*

Tender woody perennial
Height
*24 to 36 inches
(60 to 90 cm)*
Spread
24 inches (60 cm)

A culinary herb with gray-green, needle-like leaves and tiny lavender flowers. It usually blooms in early winter when it's indoors. Trailing varieties look good draping over the edge of a pot.

Requirements:

Full sun. The plant's extensive roots appreciate a deep pot. Although a Mediterranean herb, rosemary sulks if it's allowed to dry out, but rots if given too much water. It also needs more frequent fertilizing than most herbs, about every three weeks during active growth. Pinch branch tips to promote dense, bushy specimens. Plants overwintering indoors are prone to mildew, but most hang on until they can be moved out the following spring. Rosemary responds well to precise, frequent snipping, which makes it a good candidate for topiaries and small standards.

~Thyme *Thymus* spp. and cvs.

Hardy perennial
Height
*1 to 12 inches
(2.5 to 30 cm)*
Spread
up to 24 inches (60 cm)

Common thyme (*T. vulgaris*) is the culinary herb, a woody little shrub with wiry stems and tiny leaves. No container herb garden should be without it, but there are other more ornamental varieties. Variegated lemon thymes, *T. x citriodorus* 'Aureus' and 'Argenteus', have leaves with yellow and silver edges, respectively. Woolly thyme (*T. praecox* 'Pseudolanuginosus') hugs the soil with tiny, felted, gray leaves—an elegant groundcover for a pale yellow or white standard rose in a black urn. There are dozens of varieties of creeping thymes (*T. serpyllum*), with white, red or rose flowers that look good spilling over the edge of a container or planted in alpine troughs.

Requirements:

Full sun; soilless mix amended with coarse sand. Roots and leaves may rot in soggy, humid conditions or if shaded by other plants.

special
container gardens

"The only limit to your garden is at the boundaries of your imagination."

~Thomas D. Church

Some of the most interesting and rewarding container gardens revolve around themes or hobbies. You can feel productive and practical harvesting vegetables on your terrace or balcony, or snipping fresh herbs from pots lining your back steps. If al fresco dinners are a summer ritual, surrounding your patio table with pots of fragrant blooms makes lingering over coffee even more enjoyable. Or maybe you want a whole new dimension: dabble with a small water garden by tending a waterlily and a few other aquatics.

Specialized gardens are fun to plan and easy to execute. And your imagination is one of the most important tools you'll use. Here are some suggestions to help you create something out of the ordinary.

Edible Gardens: Fruits and Veggies

A few containers of vegetables might not yield enough to feed a family of four, but they do allow you to savor the just-picked flavor of produce at its prime.

Growing tomatoes, lettuce, peppers and other favorites in containers also offers a few distinct advantages over tending crops in a traditional garden plot. Soil in a container is usually a few degrees warmer in spring, summer and fall, providing a longer growing season. This is important if you want to grow long-maturing peppers or tomatoes in a climate with too few reliably frost-free days. If an unexpected late spring or early fall frost threatens, you can move a pot into shelter or throw an old sheet over it. A container's mobility also makes it possible to give plants the most sun possible by moving them to the sunny patches as the light moves across your garden.

Some vegetables are ornamental, too. The pink flowers on eggplant grow into glossy purple orbs. 'Bright Lights' Swiss chard with its red, orange, white and green stalks and ruffled, glossy green leaves is worth growing even if you never take a bite of it. Other vegetables can be "dressed up" with unusual containers—hot pepper plants growing in large olive oil tins or green beans climbing an elegant obelisk. Admittedly, a young tomato plant or one near the end of its productivity isn't all that exciting to look at. I usually add an undemanding annual, such as lobelia or dahlberg daisy (*Thymophylla tenuiloba*), around the edge of the pot. However, if your aim is to have the biggest harvest possible, grow vegetables on their own so they don't need to compete for water and nutrients. (See "Pot Sizes for Vegetables" on page 103 for matching the container size to the vegetable variety.)

Plant hybridizers have expanded the range of vegetables that grow well in pots by developing more compact plants that also have high yields. We have cabbages the size of softballs and bushy cucumber plants designed for containers, and cherry tomatoes that thrive in hanging baskets. Miniature carrots are good candidates to engage kids in the garden. To find these plants, look to a general-purpose seed catalog and study the plant descriptions, looking for varieties labeled compact, bush, balcony, etc. Or if you're buying seedlings at the nursery, read the tags carefully to find out the mature size of the plant or those that are labeled for containers.

You don't need to stick exclusively to compact, dwarf vegetable varieties. I've had good luck growing indeterminate heirloom tomatoes in large terracotta pots using tall, sturdy bamboo poles tied together at the top. ("Indeterminate" means the plant is a vine that bears fruit over a longer period compared with "determinate" plants, which are bushy with fruits that usually mature all at once.) I tied most of the stems to the supports, but allowed a few to trail over the sides. Large containers accommodate full-size pole beans, too.

Vegetables have similar requirements to other container plants with a few exceptions. They need a richer potting soil—add compost, packaged manure or good garden loam to light potting or soilless mixes. Not all vegetables love the heat: keep roots of peas, spinach, lettuces and radishes cool by using well-insulated containers, or grow them during the cooler days of spring and late summer/early fall. Maintain a careful watering routine—vegetables need a stress-free life if they're going to get down to the business of making peppers and potatoes—and feed them with an appropriate synthetic or organic fertilizer. Leafy vegetables require slightly more nitrogen; fruiting vegetables need more phosphorus; root vegetables like a bit more potassium. Don't overdo it, however. If in doubt, just use a diluted, balanced soluble fertilizer on a biweekly basis.

We want our vegetables to be healthy and productive for as long as possible, so it's not wise to crowd them. Follow spacing guidelines on seed packets for plants like carrots, beets and onions; for larger plants such as peppers, beans and tomatoes, usually one plant per pot is best. Radishes grow quickly and get by with very little soil. They, along with early-maturing leaf lettuces, are good candidates to plant with slower growing peppers, eggplants and tomatoes.

Strawberry Gardens Forever

Although it's possible to grow blueberries and gooseberries in containers, strawberries are much simpler. They even have a container that bears their name: the strawberry jar. Made of terra cotta or glazed earthenware, strawberry jars are taller than wide with evenly spaced openings, called "pockets," running up and down the sides, ideal for strawberries, which send out runners. The best-designed containers have pockets that jut out from the side—almost like little bowls. These hold water near plant roots better than jars with slits or circles punched in the sides.

> ## Pot Sizes for Vegetables
> - Tomatoes, zucchini, melons, eggplant, potatoes: five-gallon (20-L) pots
> - Peas, beans, peppers : three-gallon (12-L) pots
> - Carrots (choose short varieties), cabbage: pots at least 12 inches (30 cm) deep
> - Beets, broccoli, cucumber, lettuce: pots at least eight inches (20 cm) deep
> - Swiss chard, onions, radishes, spinach: pots at least six inches (15 cm) deep

The method for planting a strawberry jar is similar to filling a hanging basket. Fill the container with a planting mix that contains soil and coarse sand (for drainage and stability) until it reaches the bottom of the first row of openings. Insert plants, roots first, through the holes and add more soil until the next row of holes. A few small stones or dampened sphagnum moss around the base of plants keep them firmly in place.

Alpine strawberries don't grow runners like traditional strawberry plants do. Round bowl shapes show off these exceptionally perky plants with their three-part, serrated leaves and white flowers that dangle overhead. Alpine strawberries are small, but with an intense, concentrated flavor. They're well worth growing because the tiny berries aren't readily available in stores. Best of all, plants are productive all summer, not just in June, which is when most traditional strawberries bear. A pot growing in the center of a patio table means you'll be eating cornflakes al fresco most mornings. All strawberries need wintering over in a protected area such as a garage or shed.

 ## Herb Gardens

Some of the most enthusiastic and committed container gardeners started with a pot or two of kitchen herbs. Herbs are some of the most forgiving container plants because many are native to the lean soils and hot climate of the Mediterranean. Growing your favorites near the kitchen door or barbecue ensures they're close at hand and means you have a steady supply of fresh, tasty herbs. Several are tender perennials—bay, rosemary, scented geraniums, for example—that can spend winter indoors. You can enjoy them year-round. And for heat lovers like basil, life in a pot means plants can be whisked to a protected area if frost threatens.

Many herbs are highly ornamental, with attractive foliage and interesting textures that make them good candidates for mixed containers of flowering plants. Consider using a trailing rosemary for the edge of a pot or hanging basket instead of ubiquitous English ivy, or use curly parsley, silvery sage or green-and-white apple mint with colorful flowers. The tall, feathery stems and interesting seed heads of dill make an arresting accent plant in a large container.

Most herbs tolerate crowded growing conditions, but grow more lustily when given adequate soil around their roots that's quick to drain, but holds some moisture. Don't tgive tarragon, rosemary or winter savory in anything smaller than a 12-inch (30-cm) deep pot—their roots need to stretch out. Although herbs don't require as frequent feeding as flowering and fruiting plants, they do benefit from the occasional dose of a diluted, water-soluble balanced fertilizer. Basil needs more frequent feeding, probably because its big leaves are frequently snipped off for batches of pesto and tomato sauces. Feeding it encourages the production of more leaves.

Herbal Hints

Rosemary (*Rosmarinus officinalis*)

This tender perennial is native to the Mediterranean, which usually indicates drought-tolerance—but rosemary is anything but tolerant when it comes to water. Never let it dry out completely, but beware of overcompensating with too much water: soggy soil spells doom. Plants overwintered indoors sometimes develop powdery mildew, a disfiguring condition that's rarely fatal. (You can control its spread by removing affected leaves, if there aren't too many, or by giving the plants a light shower now and then.) Rosemaries are less susceptible to mildews and molds if they have as much direct sunlight as possible, good air circulation and are kept away from forced-air heat registers. To increase the level of humidity around the plants, set pots on pebbles in a tray with water halfway up the layer of pebbles. I prefer this method to misting foliage regularly with water. I winter over several rosemaries, and sometimes they look dreadfully bedraggled by late winter, but they perk up and shed the fungus once they return outdoors.

Herbal Standards

Woody herbs, such as rosemary, myrtle (*Myrtus communis*) and scented geranium (*Pelargonium* spp. and cvs.), are easy to train into standards. Standards are plants with a single, tall straight stem with foliage, usually trimmed into a sphere, on top. Buy a young plant with a strong, central stem. Insert a thin bamboo stake in the soil near the stem and tie it loosely to the stake. (The stake should be slightly shorter than the ultimate height of the standard.) Snip off the leaves near the bottom of the stem, but allow the tip to continue growing along the stake. When it reaches the top of the stake, pinch the tip, and continue pinching it back periodically. This prompts more branching at the top, which you can let grow into a small sphere. At this stage, you'll only need to trim the sphere's leaves to keep it tidy and dense.

Strawberry jars are ideal for a small collection of small-leaved herbs such as thyme, sage, cilantro and parsley. Plant a tuft of chives at the top.

Water Gardens

This is one time when using a pot with drainage holes is not a good idea. Containers that make good above-ground water gardens include wooden half-barrels or more decorative glazed earthenware or terra-cotta pots. Another possibility is one of the well-crafted plastic or fiberglass terra-cotta look-alikes. The larger sizes (more than two feet/60 cm in diameter) are usually manufactured without drainage holes.

If the container you want to use has drainage holes, plug and caulk them with silicon. To waterproof a wooden barrel, line it with dark plastic polyethylene (staple to the top edge and trim off the excess) or buy a preformed liner specifically made to fit inside a half-barrel. Water garden catalogs and large garden centers that sell pond supplies and plants often stock them.

Large containers keep water at a more consistent temperature, and reduce the rate of evaporation. They also allow for more plants. A half-barrel, which holds about 15 gallons (56 L), is big enough for one miniature waterlily, four

A Leafy Project

Leaf lettuces are incredibly easy to grow and wonderful to eat. The plants are pretty, too, with their ruffled or scalloped leaves, in colors ranging from plain green to deep purple to green splotched with red. A patchwork of different colors and textures in a wide, shallow terra-cotta container is a refreshing sight. Many leaf lettuce varieties are cut-and-come-again types (the catalog description or seed package will say). Cut the leaves near the base while young and new ones grow to harvestable size a few weeks later. Sow seeds for four or five different varieties, choosing a range of colors, leaf shapes and flavors (mild, peppery, buttery, nutty). Find a large, shallow pot—something 8 inches (20 cm) deep and at least 18 inches (45 cm) round is ideal (or build a wooden container) and plant according to package instructions. You can mix them all together to make your own mesclun mix or plant in stripes or patterns for an edible version of carpet bedding. Leaf lettuces prefer cool temperatures and part shade. Feed cut-and-come-again types diluted fish emulsion or a soluble fertilizer every two weeks.

or five oxygenating plants, two or three floating plants, three or four small goldfish and two or three water snails. Each type of flora and fauna has a role in keeping your mini ecosystem healthy: the snails clean the sides of the barrel; the fish eat insects (mosquito larvae like stagnant water); oxygenating plants keep the water clean for the fish and snails; and floating plants provide shelter for fish and shade the water surface from too much sun, which causes algae to form on the surface.

Grow marginal, or emergent, water plants in terra-cotta pots or plastic baskets. Use heavy loam—never peat moss, perlite or vermiculite, which easily floats to the surface—when potting up water plants. Even with heavy loam, you'll need to cover the surface with coarse gravel to prevent soil from floating away. The pots of marginal plants are submerged in the water and the plants rise above water level. Oxygenating plants are also planted in pots, but both the pot and the plant rest below water. Floating plants, the third type of water plants, don't grow in pots at all, but float along the water. Waterlilies, iris and other flowering plants need full sun to bloom.

Tips for a Container Water Garden

- Fill the container the day before planting and adding fish to let the water come to air temperature and the chlorine dissipate.
- Water potted water plants thoroughly before immersing them in the container.
- Some marginal plants like to have their roots well below water level, others just below the water's surface. Check the plant label or consult a water gardening book for more precise information. The measurement given indicates the distance the surface of the soil—not the bottom of the pot—is below the water. You can adjust the pot height by placing it on bricks or on empty, inverted pots.
- Aquatic plants need fertilizing too, but they're fed with tablets inserted into their pots, not with water-soluble or granular products. Water-garden supply stores and large nurseries carry the tablets.
- Fish and waterlilies don't like to be near moving water such as fountains. If you want to include a bubbler or small fountain in your container by means of a recirculating pump, you'll have to forgo these delights.
- When the water level drops due to evaporation, add more water slowly and at the side of the container. This way you won't disturb the soil or fish.

Choosing the Right Water Plants

When shopping for water plants, it's important to keep the three categories in mind—too many marginal plants, even dwarf varieties, in a container will crowd out everything else. Floaters multiply quickly, so you'll want just a few. Below are a few basic choices to consider.

Marginal Plants
- Blue flag (*Iris versicolor*)
- Dwarf cattail (*Typha minima*)
- Dwarf papyrus (*Cyperus profiler*)
- Dwarf waterlilies (*Nymphaea* spp. and cvs.)
- Marsh marigold (*Caltha palustris*)

- Pickerel rush (*Pontederia cordata*)
- Yellow flag (*Iris pseudacorus*)

Oxygenating Plants
- Arrowhead (*Sagittaria* spp.)
- Canadian pondweed (*Elodea canadensis*) Note: pondweed is very invasive; don't let it escape into natural waterways.
- Water violet (*Hottonia palustris*)

Floating Plants
- Frogbit (*Hydrocharis morsus-ranae*)
- Water fern (*Azolla filiculoides*)
- Water hyacinth (*Eichhornia crassipes*)
- Water lettuce (*Pistia stratiotes*)

Small Delights: Alpine Gardens

If you want to enter into the charming world of alpines, choose a terra-cotta or rough concrete bowl. Some creative types make their own free-form concrete containers for an even more natural-looking setting. Natural materials and organic shapes enhance miniature landscapes created with small rock-garden plants.

True alpines are plants native to mountainous areas above the tree line, but the term is loosely applied to any hardy perennial that's less than six inches (15 cm) tall, likes well-drained soil and doesn't spread too vigorously. Alpines require soil that can stay moist without being waterlogged: use two parts potting mix that includes soil and one part very coarse, gritty sand. Most alpines bloom in the spring or early summer and need full sun. If you're using a new container, age it by painting the surface with yogurt or buttermilk and mist daily until the surface blooms with the desirable green mold that will make everyone think your alpine collection has been around for decades.

Fill your container almost to the rim and mound it up slightly in the center. This prevents water from collecting around the crowns of the plants, which are especially susceptible to rot. Choose a variety of cushion- and mat-forming plants, and space them in the container so that the dainty attributes of each can be appreciated. Some common rock garden plants are found in the

Sedum, *Saxifraga*, *Dianthus*, *Campanula* and *Gentiana* genera. Mulch the exposed soil surface with a layer of coarse sand or pea gravel. A few small, flat rocks, partially submerged among the plants, are an attractive addition as long as the end result doesn't look like giant chocolate chips dropped from the sky. Monitor water carefully—alpines need moisture but detest soggy conditions. Alpines grow slowly, so fertilize them much less frequently than other container plants—once or twice a year at most. Prune if plants get leggy or start to crowd each other. These diminutive treasures are extremely hardy, which means extra protection over winter is unnecessary as long as the plants don't get waterlogged during freeze-thaw cycles.

 ## Spring-Flowering Bulbs

A pot of colorful spring bulbs at the front door is a joyful sight after the monochromatic shades of winter. Plant tulips, daffodils, crocus, small alliums, muscari and hyacinths in the fall in containers, placing them so they're almost touching, and the tips of the bulbs are an inch (2.5 cm) below the rim of the pot. Water well and store in a cool, dark location over winter. A garage, unheated basement or cold cellar is fine. Check the pots occasionally, watering if the soil is dry. When shoots begin to pop out in early spring, move them out into partial shade and enjoy the show.

If you lack storage space or forget to pot up some bulbs in the fall, it's perfectly okay to cheat and buy pots already in bud or bloom at the garden center or greengrocer in the spring. Place the pots in a decorative container, and camouflage the plastic rims with sphagnum moss. Bulbs grown this way are too exhausted to be forced a consecutive year, but you can plant them in the garden where they may recuperate enough to bloom again the following year. Let the foliage die off naturally; removing it prematurely robs bulbs of energy that helps them form next year's flowers.

 ## Fragrant Gardens

A potted garden filled with fragrant flowers is one of the simplest to make. The key is determining what plants are truly effusive with their fragrance—not so stingy that in order to catch a whiff of their scent you must grow at least three dozen and position your nose an inch above the blooms, breathe deeply and concentrate.

Catalog writers (and garden book and magazine writers, too) are often overly enthusiastic and optimistic about the fragrance factor of flowers. On the next page is a list of the most fragrant flowers and foliage—annuals, bulbs,

Overleaf: Here's a gardener who's not afraid to use color, and lots of it. The back deck overflows with pots and planters of all sizes, grouped together for maximum impact. Healthy pansies, fuchsias, petunias and geraniums in cheery pinks, purples and lilac put on an exuberant show all summer.

Right: The temperature extremes and ▶ drying winds common to balcony and rooftop gardens are challenges, but not insurmountable ones. The large amount of soil the wooden half-barrels (opposite page and right) hold help protect plant roots from fluctuating temperatures. The sturdy zinnias can stand up to the wind and hot sun, too.

◀ *Left*: Three small square planters clustered at the base of a large concrete pot create a tiered effect, as well as a pleasing contrast of shapes and textures. The large concrete pot holds 'Blackie' and 'Marguerita' sweet potato vines (*Ipomoea batatus* cvs.) and salmon million bells (*Calibrachoa* cv.). Variegated and purple sage plants grow in the lower center planter.

Right: Compact cultivars of red and ▶ white nicotiana sparkle in a small tabletop arrangement. Variegated helichrysum and English ivy add foliage interest. The gardener is careful not to let the plants obscure the intriguing design on the front of the unusual metal pot.

◀ *Left*: Stacked terra-cotta pots in graduated sizes mark the entrance to the author's side garden. A wooden dowel runs through the pots' drainage holes to keep the structure stable. The smallest pot holds a gazania daisy, and various creeping thymes and sedums fill the middle and bottom pots. The pyramid of pots requires careful watering because the top two dry out more rapidly than the bottom pot.

vines, tender perennials—that will be noticed on a summer evening as you relax outside enjoying the warm night air. Set containers close to seating areas—a few feet above ground, if practical—to maximize their olfactory impact. By placing scented plants along a path or beside steps, you increase your chances of brushing or rustling the plants as you pass by, which releases even more of their fragrance. Or place a window box of fragrant choices outside a bedroom window where the scent can waft over you on night breezes. Balconies and small, enclosed garden areas are some of the best places for a scented garden because enclosed areas confine the scents, making them more noticeable.

 ## Hummingbird and Butterfly Havens

One of the joys of gardening is watching visitors' reactions to all of your efforts. Some of my favorite visitors are hummingbirds and butterflies. If you want to make your container garden a part of their route, include a few of these plants, which provide the nectar they like:

- Impatiens
- Petunia
- Nasturtium (*Tropaeolum majus*)
- Zinnia, especially pom-pom types
- Marigolds (*Tagetes* spp. and cvs.)
- Verbena
- Fuchsia
- Calendula
- Heliotrope (*Heliotropium arborescens*)
- Nicotiana
- Salvia (*S. splendens*)

 ## Rose Gardens

Roses are good candidates for containers, as long as some thought is given when choosing from the hundreds available. Hybrid teas are lovely, but most are magnets for disease, high-maintenance and less hardy than the equally beautiful miniature, China, hybrid perpetual, polyantha and smaller Explorer roses (bred in Canada to withstand especially cold winters), which are better suited to containers. Plant pale pink miniature roses and blue trailing lobelia in a wicker basket for a soft, romantic effect, or splurge on a rose standard (floribundas and polyanthas are good choices) and site it in a prominent location in your best pot. To overwinter, place the rose in its container against the

- Daffodils (Jonquil group)
- Dianthus (*Dianthus* spp. and cvs.)
- *Gladiolus callianthus*
- Grape hyacinths (*Muscari* spp.)
- Heliotrope (*Heliotropium arborescens*)
- *Hosta plantaginea* and *H.* 'Royal Standard'
- Hyacinths (*Hyacinthus orientalis*)
- Jasmine (*Jasminum* spp.)
- Lavender (*Lavendula* spp.)
- Lilies, especially *Lilium regale*, and varieties in the Oriental, aurelian and trumpet categories
- Mignonette (*Reseda odorata*); nothing to look at, but highly perfumed
- *Nicotiana alata*
- Old-fashioned sweetpeas, such as *Lathyrus cupani*
- Petunias, the big, floppy old-fashioned types are best
- Small-leaved basil (*Ocimum basilicum* 'Siam Queen' and 'Spicy Globe')
- Sweet alyssum (*Lobularia maritima*)

warmest wall in an unheated garage. Set the pot in a large garbage bag and loosely fold the top over the soil, up around the base of the rose. Remove leaves as they fall and water occasionally during dormancy so the soil doesn't dry out completely. In spring, move the pot back outdoors and prune lightly to trigger new growth; resume feeding.

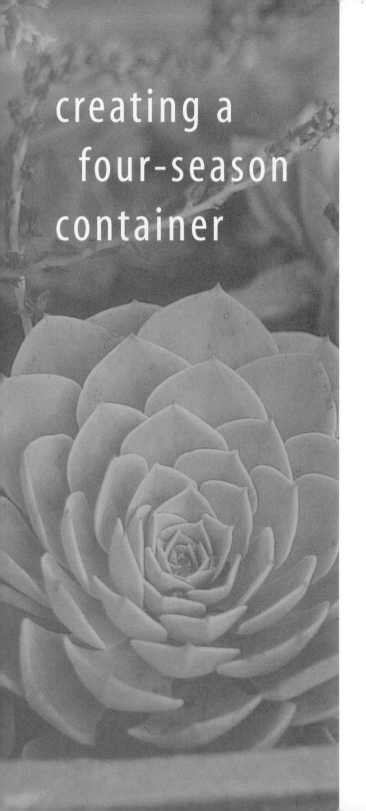

creating a four-season container

9

"If we had no winter,

spring would not be so pleasant."

~Anne Bradstreet

Watching a garden evolve as the seasons unfold is one of gardening's greatest pleasures. This process doesn't often happen in container gardens because they're usually planted at the beginning of summer and dismantled in the fall.

But there is no rule that says a container planting is only a one-season wonder, even where winters are long and brutal. Of course, creating a new arrangement of plants for spring, summer, fall and winter in every pot, box and basket in your landscape would be impractical—as well as costly and exhausting—but the enjoyment of a year-round, seasonal showpiece in one or two key locations is immensely gratifying. If you have a large container that will withstand the ravages of winter, place it near a high-traffic site—at the front entrance or outside a sliding door to your patio—some prime spot where it can be seen as you enter and leave the house or be viewed from indoors.

Planting a four-season container is different from the concept of overwintering plants (see "Overwintering Plants" on page 129). Wintering over involves permanent plantings maintained from year to year, such as tender plants brought indoors over winter, a collection of hardy perennials in a balcony planter, or a potted shrub or tree that goes dormant. Some may be moved into storage, others wrapped or left in situ, but the goal is to help them survive the winter. We don't count on them to delight us with their floral and foliage display during every season. A four-season approach relies on an evolving, changing plant scene within one decorative container—much like what goes on in the surrounding landscape. It involves replanting the designated container with plants appropriate to the season—fresh, new looks in spring, summer, autumn and winter.

I use a 30-inch (75-cm) tall cast-iron urn with a rusty brown finish for my ode to the four seasons. In hindsight, I wish I'd chosen a different shape. Although attractive, the classic, large urn doesn't offer a generous enough planting surface—the top is a mere 18 inches (45 cm) across. But before I describe what I plant in the urn that flanks our front door, here are a few tips to simplify the process, regardless of your site and container.

Tips for Creating a Four-Season Display

- Use large plants, most of which are in bud or bloom. The aim is to make the display look full and finished from the start, because spring and fall vignettes will be on stage for only six to eight weeks, depending on the weather.
- To add instant height, create an elevated planting section that sits in the center, a few inches above the top of the container. To do this, first fill the container with soil until it's about two inches (5 cm) below the rim. Take a

black or brown plastic or fiberboard pot about six to eight inches (15 to 20 cm) in diameter and press the bottom two inches (7 cm) into the surface of the soil to anchor it and keep it from tipping over when it's planted. Either plant your tall specimen plant directly into this smaller, raised pot, or slip in a slightly smaller pot already containing the desired plant. Forced tulips in the spring, a canna in the summer, ornamental grasses in the fall—all are tall accent plants that look even more dramatic when elevated this way. Just slip the plant out of the raised pot when you want a change. To disguise the sides of the raised pot, position other plants around it when you're filling the rest of the container.

- It's unnecessary to completely strip the container at the end of each season. Some plants can bridge the seasons. For example, trailing English ivy (*Hedera helix*) planted in spring can remain over summer and into fall, if you like. Daffodils planted in early spring fade before pansies do, but the pansies peter out by midsummer and you'll need to plug in something else. You get the idea: replace plants as needed, always keeping in mind your overall color scheme. Have a few small plants waiting in the wings to fill in bare spots as they occur.

- Sphagnum moss provides a finishing touch and hides bare stems, gaps or exposed rims of plant pots or containers. Moisten it, squeeze out excess water and tuck in chunks where a little camouflage is needed. The moss also helps support floppy stems and conserves moisture in the soil.

- In some climates a small evergreen can provide year-round foliage, while the plants around it may change according to what's in bloom. An upright juniper adds vertical interest and bulk—and is hardier than broadleaf evergreens like boxwood or holly that might desiccate in drying winter winds or not survive exceptionally harsh winters.

 ## Salute to Spring

Consider using non-traditional spring colors to set your container apart. I use oranges, reds and golds instead of the predictable pastel pinks, lilacs, pale yellows and white common to most spring gardens. A jolt of bright color after the drab grays, duns and dirty white of fading winter months is a welcome sight for me.

One April, I started with forced bulbs—small, white daffodils, tall burnt-orange parrot tulips, bright yellow double tulips—burgundy primroses (*Primula vulgaris* cultivar) and yellow globes of double-flowered ranunculus (*R. asiaticus* cultivar). A smattering of blue grape hyacinths (*Muscari latifolium*) acted as a foil to the hot colors. Swags of soft gray-green variegated English ivy spilled over the edge. When the daffodils and grape hyacinths began to fade,

I replaced them with solid yellow pansies and pansies with maroon-and-yellow faces. After about six weeks, the tulips had faded and the weather was warm enough for summer planting. The pansies were still okay, but because they usually look bedraggled by the end of June, I didn't count on them to carry through until fall. Of course, ivy lasts forever. If I didn't need it in my summer scheme, I could have moved the plants elsewhere. English ivy is most forgiving and always eager to fling its lacy mantle wherever it's planted.

Other good plants for spring planting schemes are cyclamen (*C. persicum* or other hardier species), cut branches from spring-flowering shrubs (such as forsythia, pussy willows or viburnum), violets, tall crown imperials fritillaria (*Fritillaria imperialis*) and forget-me-nots (*Myosotis sylvatica*).

If you have trouble finding potted bulbs in interesting colors at your local garden center or nursery, visit a small florist or greengrocer. They often make weekly buying trips to the local wholesale market, and they might be willing to bring in what you want if they know ahead of time. If you're *really* thinking ahead, force your own bulbs, starting the process the preceding fall.

Maintenance

Forced bulbs, ranunculus, primroses and pansies don't require hardening-off—they like cool temperatures, although several nights of unexpected hard frost or a covering of snow will probably set them back a bit—in cases of uncooperative spring weather, throw an old sheet over the top for temporary protection.

Deadhead faded blooms on bulbs, pansies and primroses. Once the bulbs have finished flowering completely, you can replant them in your garden, although it may take them a couple of years to recover from being forced into early bloom. When transplanting forced bulbs to the garden, let the foliage remain so it ripens naturally—this process feeds subsequent years' blooms. Water the bulbs after planting, and again if the spring is exceptionally dry. Primroses, as well as violets, forget-me-nots and other spring-blooming hardy perennials, can be moved into the garden as well.

 # Summer Splendors

The myriad flowers available for a container in summer are as endless as we wish the season to be. In my case, I continued with hot colors, concentrating on bronzes and corals. Out went the spent tulips, ranunculus, primroses and a couple of the ivies. My summer plants included a tall New Zealand flax (*Phormium tenax* 'Atropurpurea') with deep bronze, sturdy, sword-shape leaves, which I inserted into the small, elevated container that once held tulips. Nearly upstaging the New Zealand flax was a large, multi-colored coleus

(*Solenostemon scutellarioides* 'Yellow Duckfoot'). Its heavily mottled leaves—burgundy and salmon in the center, yellow and green on the edges—was a real stunner. Filling in and spilling over the rest of the urn were gold bidens, coral 'Gartenmeister Bonsteadt' fuchsia, which has purplish stems and leaves, a pastel peach cigar plant (*Cuphea ignea*) and long strings of 'Illumination' vinca vine (*Vinca major*), which has gold leaves with wide, green edges. The maroon- and yellow-faced pansies continued to be real stalwarts, blooming their little heads off until fall.

Maintenance

Deadheading, careful watering and biweekly feeding with a 15-30-15 water-soluble fertilizer mixed at half strength kept the urn full of blooms during a hot, humid summer. The coleus got a bit top-heavy and the bidens browned-out, but judicial trimming helped.

Fall Follies

It's often difficult to uproot a summer display to make way for fall's show because many of the plants are still in good shape. However, summer containers have usually had a long run—from early June to early September—and the chance to celebrate the bounty of autumn wins out. I usually eschew the traditional colors of this season as well—the trees and shrubs in the garden offer plenty of gold, scarlet, russet and orange. Instead, I filled the urn with a medium-tall cultivar of miscanthus, an ornamental grass that shines in autumn, a tiny pink chrysanthemum, pink pansies, a cool blue Michaelmas daisy (*Aster novi-belgii* cultivar) and a sedum with glaucous or purple foliage and pink flowers (*S. sieboldii* or *S.* 'Vera Jameson'). Another neat idea is to make a colorful "pincushion" with small ornamental kales (*Brassica oleracea* cultivars) in alternating pinks and whites. Plant them tightly in a raised bun shape in a large-diameter container. The look is tidy and formal, and an interesting contrast to the blowsy abundance of fall.

Other container plants for fall are tall sedums such as *Sedum* 'Autumn Joy' or purple coneflower (*Echinacea purpurea*), Japanese anemone (*A.* × *hybrida*), miniature sunflowers, black-eyed Susans (*Rudbeckia fulgida*) and cut branches of Chinese lanterns (*Physalis alkekengi*) or bittersweet (*Celastrus scandens*).

Maintenance

Ornamental cabbages or kale deepen in color as temperatures drop and seem to last forever, but they eventually succumb after a few hard frosts and wet snowfalls. They do not die gracefully, but become unsightly mushy mounds with an odor reminiscent of, well, stale cabbage. Remove them before the container soil freezes solid so you don't have to see—or smell—them all winter. If you use corn stalks for something tall, don't be surprised if raccoons or squirrels stop by for a snack.

Even though the end of the growing season is nigh, late-blooming plants keep flowering if they're deadheaded, carefully watered and lightly fertilized until the snow falls.

Winter Wonders

Most containers created for the winter months are more of an outdoor floral arrangement than a collection of living plants. Let's be realistic, unless you live in a moderate climate or in the south, most plants are dormant when temperatures stay below freezing for weeks on end. There are attractive plants in our garden during winter—holly, boxwood, pieris, conifers—but they have a tough time surviving in exposed containers in northern climates. But that doesn't mean you can't use cut branches of these winter beauties and many others to create a vivid and long-lasting arrangement for a large container that will carry you over until spring. I leave most of the soil in the bottom of a container after removing fall's plants; pushing the ends of branches in soil anchors them far more than leaving them loose in the container.

Winter containers call for an appreciation of all the variations in color, form and texture that evergreen branches offer. I like to use plenty of soft, flexible evergreen specimens, such as white pine, so the overall look is relaxed and graceful. A container filled with upright branches of spruce and boxwood looks stiff and dense.

Contorted branches or those with colorful bark from deciduous trees and shrubs are also good candidates for a winter container arrangement. The lingering berries and seed heads found on some shrubs are intriguing, too. Most often used are red-twig dogwood (*Cornus alba*), but there are plenty of other equally good candidates. Japanese kerria (*K. japonica*) has bright green branches year-round and the peeling, corky bark of burning-bush (*Euonymus alata*), sometimes with small, red seed capsules, is equally attractive. Hollies, curly willow (*Salix babylonica* 'Tortuosa'), corkscrew hazel (*Corylus avellana* 'Contorta'), bittersweet, dried hydrangea flowerheads, fat rosehips from shrub roses and winterberry branches (*Ilex verticillata*) are other worthy candidates. Take a close look at the trees and shrubs around you. Sometimes simple twiggy and multi-stemmed branches can be interesting when grouped in a container. Look for interesting patterns of crisscrossing branches. Let branches lean at different angles and stagger their heights.

When harvesting material for your winter container, take only a few branches from each plant, and cut where a missing branch or two won't be noticed—you don't want to ruin next spring's display. Make clean cuts close to the base of the branch; don't cut into the main branch, but don't leave a stub either.

At Christmas time, dress up a winter container with hard fruits like apples and pears. Impale each fruit on the end of a green 18-inch (45-cm) bamboo stake and stick the other end in the container deeply enough so the fruit looks like it's nestled among the boughs and branches. If it sticks too far above the greenery, you'll have "lollipops" on a stick. Depending on the temperature, wind and sun factors, you can sometimes create the effect of frozen dew drops by misting branches. You may want to string tiny white lights through the arrangement for an even more festive look, but I prefer to let a white uplight shed soft light on a winter container if I feel the need to illuminate it in the evenings. Most containers are viewed from close up, as well as from the street, and strings of holiday lights among the greenery are a distraction during daylight.

Maintenance

Usually all that's required is the removal of the dried-out, brown evergreen branches. Spraying with water or an anti-desiccant may help evergreen branches stay bright green. Berries on branches and rosehips fall off or are snacked on by birds, but that's not the end of the world. Fresh fruit usually lasts only a couple of weeks outdoors.

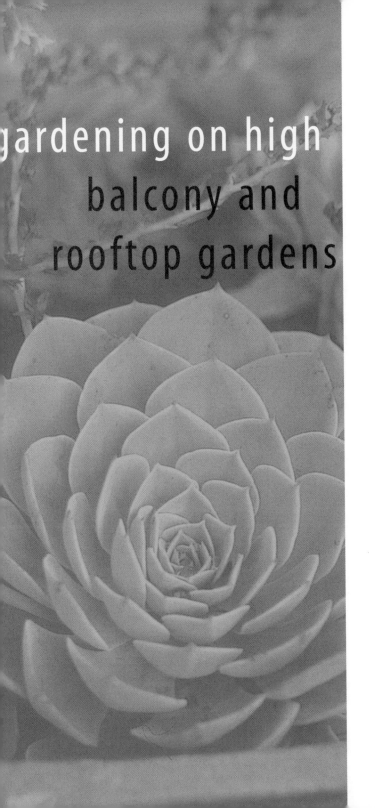

gardening on high
balcony and rooftop gardens

10

*"The tiniest garden
is often the loveliest."*

~Vita Sackville-West

rowing plants on balconies and rooftops has a few additional challenges. To create a sky-high oasis means first taming an exposed site—one that offers little protection from the elements. The trees, hedges and fences in ground-level gardens that filter the wind, buffer temperature extremes and temper the sun aren't part of the landscape a few stories up. Balconies and rooftops are surrounded by buildings that cast impenetrable shade—sometimes for half a day or more—and merciless winds that barrel down between buildings, upending pots and stripping off leaves.

Of course, if you crave flowers, leaves, trees and vines outside your sliding glass doors, you're not going to let these minor inconveniences discourage you. High-rise gardening is not for the timid or the pessimistic, but with careful planning, research and plant choices, it's possible to have a healthy, abundant high-rise garden.

Some Practical Considerations

Before you begin lugging bags of potting soil up the elevator, determine if the surface you'll be gardening on will withstand the weight of containers, soil and water. (And you might want to measure the elevator before taking delivery of large trees or broad shrubs.) The combined weight of these items is not insignificant: a wooden half-barrel filled with moist soil weighs 200 pounds (99 kg). Allow a safety margin, especially if you're going to have parties with a dozen people line dancing on your roof or balcony. Always check with a building manager or superintendent for restrictions and weight limits before adding more than a few containers. Consult a structural engineer if your plans are truly ambitious. His or her services will cost far less than hiring a lawyer after your half dozen barrels cause your balcony to pull away from the side of the building.

Place the heaviest pots along weight-bearing walls, normally the outer walls on a roof. If your roof garden plans are extensive, you may need to have a steel beam and deck joists installed to span the roof and transfer the weight to the outer, weight-bearing walls. Lay decking in sections over the joists so any subsequent roof repairs won't require dismantling the entire floor.

Water not only contributes to the weight of a balcony garden, its mere presence can damage a balcony floor or find its way into the apartment or balcony below when it drains from pots. Consider installing a drainage system to take excess water out to downspouts, drains or eaves, and suspend a second floor of wood decking over top.

There are ways to reduce the weight of planted containers. Use a soilless mix or one with a high proportion of peat moss, vermiculite or perlite—these weigh less than soil. Unfortunately, they also dry out more quickly and plants require more frequent feeding. Choose containers made of lightweight plastic, wood or fiberglass. Plastic and fiberglass have the additional benefit of being more moisture-retentive than heavier terra cotta and stone. However, plastic containers are sometimes a false economy because they become brittle when exposed to a few seasons of sun and frost. And their lightness can be hazardous on exceptionally windy days.

For short-term plantings (lasting a season or two), crushed plastic pots or Styrofoam chips in the bottom third of large pots reduces the amount of soil needed. Place landscape cloth over top to prevent soil from filtering down into the layer of filler material. I don't recommend this treatment for long-term plantings, such as trees and shrubs, or vegetables that benefit from a large, healthy root system, like tomatoes or squash. But flowering annuals won't notice.

Anchor all small balcony boxes, hanging baskets, trellises, obelisks and wall-mounted containers securely. (Remember those lawyers' fees.)

The relative isolation of a balcony or rooftop garden means gaining access to the site and storing materials are key issues. How many bags of topsoil are you prepared to carry across your white broadloom? And then there's the dilemma of discarding depleted soil, along with the plants, at the end of the season. If you're composting, this won't be an issue for you. But compost bins take up space, of which you have a limited amount. Don't forget to leave room for pruners, a hose, watering can, extra soil, fertilizer, etc. Some avid balcony gardeners with lots of plants use a wet/dry vacuum to clean up spills—soil and water—and to suck up plant debris during fall cleanups. At least a vacuum cleaner is smaller than a lawn mower, one accoutrement you won't need to store on the roof.

What to Plant?

Once you know that your flooring is up to the stresses of weight and water, and you've decided on other practicalities, you can move on to more pleasant decisions: what to plant? The sky's the limit, although you'd be wise to pass on plants with fragile blooms and big leaves, such as petunias, roses and hostas, which can easily be shredded by high winds. Plants with sturdy, leathery leaves like those on mandevilla and English ivy; thin, flexible leaves found on ornamental grasses and daylilies; and low-growing plants such as portulaca, thyme and sedums stand up to the rigors of high living. If shrubs and trees are part of the design, choose iron-hardy specimens with open forms and small leaves. Siberian peashrub (*Caragana arborescens*), serviceberry (*Amelanchier* spp. and cvs.), amur maple (*Acer ginnala*), cutleaf staghorn sumac (*Rhus typhina* 'Dissecta'), crabapples (*Malus* spp. and cvs.) Russian olive

(*Elaeagnus angustifolia*), sea buckthorn (*Hippophae rhamnoides*) and mock orange (*Philadelphus* spp. and cvs.) are a few candidates. Young, single-stemmed trees may need staking for a year or two. If you don't want to look at stakes and ties, choose other plants to give your garden height: ornamental grasses or vines on obelisks or trellises, such as black-eyed Susan vine (*Thunburgia alata*), morning glories—or even scarlet runner beans (*Phaseolus coccineus*) with pretty red blossoms and edible green beans.

Study the amount of sun your balcony or roof receives in spring, and again in midsummer. An adjacent wall may mean plants get strong sun for part of the day and solid shade the rest of the time. If necessary—and allowable—paint the outdoor surfaces white to increase the amount of reflected light. Temperature extremes intensify above ground. Roots may cook in small black plastic pots sitting on a southwest-facing balcony. Choose plants that tolerate heat (check the information in Chapter 7, "Plants for the Potted Garden," for suggestions) and plant them in large containers—soil is a great insulator. In winter, the wind is stronger and the temperatures are colder several stories above ground; a tree that survives in a container at the ground-level condominium below yours may not survive 15 floors above.

 ## Design

Obviously, space is at a premium, especially on balconies, where you'll not only have plants, but likely a table and chairs, and perhaps a barbecue and bicycles. Avoid prickly, thorny specimens in tight quarters—you don't want to be snagged on the way to the chaise longue. Look for plants that have interesting form and foliage, as well as pretty flowers. Let two or three plants act as focal points, and group a collection of smaller plants nearby.

One way to increase the available gardening space is to use your abundant vertical space and plant vines. They take up scant floor space, but offer a bower of beauty. Most grow quickly, provide plenty of color, and some are fragrant (sweetpeas, honeysuckle, jasmine). Attach ready-made trellis to a wall or nail the bottom eight inches (20 cm) of a trellis to the back of a planting box. Eye hooks screwed into a wall with thin wire or twine strung through them is another way to make a climbing apparatus for vines.

Several vines growing on a large, sturdy screen or wide trellis can be used to diffuse the wind, filter the sun, provide privacy from the neighbors or hide the compost bins, stored bicycles, etc. Make sure there are open spaces in the screen so some wind passes through (a solid surface will create another pocket of turbulence), and anchor it firmly to the floor and wall in several spots. Grow the vines in an attached planter at the base or in pots clustered at the bottom.

Carefully tie vines to supports as they grow to prevent long stems from snapping off in the wind. Use a figure-eight loop and soft cotton or jute twine; lengths of pantyhose work, too, but given the proximity of most balcony gardens, you or your neighbors may not want to gaze at torn hosiery all summer.

The smaller the space, the bigger impact the colors you choose for plants and containers will have. White and pale-colored flowers lighten up a small space, making it seem larger. If the balcony is used mainly in the evenings, an all-white garden is lovely. For a cozy, dramatic, enveloping mood, choose a dark, rich palette—purple, blue, maroon, hot pink—tempered with plenty of rich, green foliage.

More Design Ideas

- If a breathtaking view of the skyline brought you to a particular high-rise apartment or condominium, don't obscure it with plants. Position containers to frame the view, not block it.
- Use structures to enhance a rooftop or balcony garden. The reflections of a mirror mounted on a wall, framed by a vine-covered trellis perhaps, make a small space seem larger. Position the mirror so it reflects greenery, not the wall of the building next door. Trompe l'oeil (literally, "fool the eye") enlivens a plain, flat wall. Trellising with a false perspective is striking, too.

Rooftop Gardens Versus Gardening on a Rooftop

The term "rooftop garden" doesn't always mean plants growing in pots and planters arranged on a flat roof. An environmental movement, especially in urban areas, encourages owners of commercial and residential buildings to plant turf grasses, wildflowers and other low-growing, drought-resistant species directly onto flat or sloping rooftops. The seeds or seedlings are planted into a shallow layer of soil that's contained in a membrane covering the entire surface. The aim is to cover as much unused roof space as possible in order to improve air quality, reflect heat and prevent storm water runoff from overloading storm sewage systems. The layer of soil and

plants on a rooftop also provides insulating qualities that keep buildings warmer in winter, cooler in summer.

These types of rooftop gardens are more common in Europe and Asia than in North America, although the number of projects on this continent increases each year. In some German cities, new industrial buildings are required to install green roofs. In Switzerland, new buildings must relocate the green space covered by the building's footprint to the roof areas. A good source for up-to-date information on the rooftop garden movement is City Farmer, an eight-year-old, not-for-profit Web site (*www.cityfarmer.org*) based in Vancouver, British Columbia, which promotes urban food production and conservation.

- The right angles and solid surfaces ubiquitous to balconies and roofs make ideal backdrops for formal plantings. Square Versailles boxes with tightly trimmed conifers or a delicately pruned Japanese maple (*Acer palmatum*) add drama and structure. Formal designs rely on symmetry and repeating motifs: a series of identically planted hanging baskets or a monochromatic color scheme reinforce a formal look.
- An informal, cottage garden–style theme is also possible on a small balcony or roof space. Camouflage the edges and surfaces of containers with mounding and trailing plants. Use shredded bark on the floor to simulate a narrow path through cozy, blowsy plantings that include a cacophony of flower shapes and colors. Plant herbs and vegetables with your flowers. Choose containers in classic shapes made from natural materials—wood or terra cotta. Screen the cityscape from view with annual vines and you'll think you've stumbled down a country path.

 ## Permanent Plantings

High-rise gardeners, bereft of the hedges, trees and shrubs that ground-level gardeners enjoy, are especially keen to grow deciduous or evergreen shrubs. Because it's impractical to bring these large specimens into a condo or apartment, these permanent plantings need to withstand the rigors of winter outdoors. If you live where winters rarely dip far below freezing, all you'll need to be concerned with is moving maturing specimens into larger pots as they grow taller and wider. In colder climates, it's a different scenario.

Even roots in ground-level containers must be able to withstand colder temperatures than their counterparts growing in the ground (see "Overwintering Plants" on page 129). Move that containerized tree up to the 10th floor and the temperature extremes are compounded. Winter winds are especially troublesome for coniferous trees and broadleaf evergreens, which transpire water through their needles and leaves throughout the year. If a rootball is frozen for long periods of time, the water it loses through transpiration can't be replaced, and the foliage dries out, turns brown and drops off.

It's not just cold temperatures and drying winds that strike down plants that spend winter in containers far above ground level—the season's inevitable freeze/thaw cycles also contribute to their demise. A few warm, sunny days in early February thaw the plant and its roots, causing it to think spring is here to stay, so the plant breaks dormancy. Of course, in most of Canada and the northern states, spring arrives two or three months after February. When the soil freezes again—as it inevitably does—any new growth triggered by the surprise thaw is killed. The stress of stopping and starting growth over and over again is too much for a woody plant, and it succumbs. Even on bitterly cold days, the sun may thaw the soil during the day, whereupon it freezes again at night. Therefore, it's crucial to keep the plant in a dormant state until it truly is spring. Big planters that hold lots of soil provide more insulation for plant roots.

Wooden containers are ideal for permanent plantings on balconies and roofs. They can be customized to fit odd-size spaces and large, permanent plantings, and wood is a good insulator. Planters for perennials need to be at least 18 inches (45 cm) deep; trees and shrubs need two-and-a-half feet (75 cm). It's easy to add casters to wooden boxes, which makes moving heavy planters much easier. Line the inside with thick sheets of Styrofoam insulation, the kind used for house insulation, or tie the sheets around the outside of containers after a hard frost. If you're using containers made from other frost-proof materials, tie insulation around their perimeter, too.

Pushing the Zones

Trees and shrubs are more expensive than other plants, and this is the time to be realistic when wintering over plants on a balcony or roof. Considering the vagaries of winter, one must always be prepared for the occasional loss. In colder parts of Canada and the U.S., choose trees and shrubs hardy to two climatic zones colder than where you live. For example, southern Toronto and Halifax are in Zone 6 on the Canadian Plant Hardiness Zone Map. (The United States uses the USDA Plant Hardiness Zone Map, and areas in Michigan, Illinois and Ohio, which have similar winter conditions to those in Toronto and Halifax, are in Zone 5 under that system.) Trees hardy to Zone 4 and colder have a better chance of surviving on a balcony or roof in these areas. Garden centers, plant catalogs and gardening reference books can confirm the hardiness zone of your garden.

However, don't be frightened off by hardiness zone ratings; there are myriad factors that affect a plant's hardiness, and winter temperature is only one. The care a plant receives the rest of the year, as well as the amount of snow cover and wind, and its orientation to the sun, all have an impact on a plant's relative hardiness. It's always worth experimenting on a small scale, especially if you come across a well-priced tree or shrub. You may be pleasantly surprised at what survives, and then you can boast to all of your gardening friends about what grows on *your* balcony. Part of the fun in gardening is experimenting and proving gardening books wrong.

More Survival Strategies

- When planting, keep the soil level low enough to accommodate a two-inch (5-cm) layer of mulch in winter.
- Select slow-growing or dwarf trees and shrubs.
- Specimens that blossom in early spring may not do well far above ground. The colder temperatures may freeze the flowers, and a lack of pollinating bees reduces yield on fruit trees.
- Pruning keeps trees within bounds, allows wind to pass through easily and reduces the weight of the container. Prune when trees are dormant or, in the case of flowering shrubs, after blooming. Treat the tree like a living sculpture, not a muffin in a tin. Step back every once in a while to check your progress. Don't be afraid to prune, but know when to stop.
- Annual feeding of mature trees is usually adequate, but if the leaves begin to yellow or the tree produces smaller leaves, supplement with another application of fertilizer during the growing season.
- As the edges of permanent plants become more pot-bound, they dry out even more quickly (the ratio of roots to soil changes). Monitor moisture levels diligently.

For more tips on growing plants year round in containers, see "Overwintering Plants" on page 129.

To Repot or Not?

As trees and shrubs grow in width and height, they'll need repotting. Signs that a plant needs repotting include soil that dries out quickly, tightly packed roots within a pot, roots protruding from drainage holes or water sitting on the soil's surface too long after watering. When moving plants to a larger pot, don't increase the pot size by more than an inch or two (2.5 to 5 cm). If the volume of soil—and accompanying moisture—around the roots increases too abruptly, plants may rot from the sudden extra moisture.

The best time to repot is when a plant is actively growing. Moisten the soil before removing it from its pot. Trim the bottom roots and loosen roots growing along the sides. Cut through any roots growing in a circle around the rootball. If you're faced with a thick, tight netting of roots, take a sharp knife and make three equally spaced vertical cuts along the sides from top to bottom. (This root brutality is to coax them to grow out into the new soil after they're replanted.)

If you end up removing a significant amount of roots while repotting, prune a corresponding amount of above-ground growth. Fewer roots mean fewer nutrients reach stems, branches and leaves. Therefore, if you remove a quarter of a plant's roots, remove a quarter of its top growth, too.

the long term
caring for
nd overwintering
container plants

11

*"Nature does not hesitate
to interfere with me,
so I do not hesitate
to tamper with it."*

~Henry Mitchell

areful watering and fertilizing have the most impact on a potted garden, but there are a few other techniques that also help plants stay healthy and hearty. When the end of another gardening season arrives, there may even be a few favorites you'll want to carry over for next year's display. The following are suggestions to keep plants thriving—for now and maybe forever.

Ongoing Care and Troubleshooting

Deadheading

Remove spent blossoms or flower stalks on annuals to keep plants tidy and promote more blooms. Nip off all of the flower parts, not just the petals. The object is to stop plants from producing seed, which triggers plants to stop flowering. Not all plants require deadheading. In some cases, the blooms drop off on their own, or are small enough and in such abundance that deadheading is unnecessary. Plants that don't need deadheading include wax begonias, browallia, cigar flower (*Cuphea ignea*), impatiens, portulaca, bacopa, black-eyed Susan vine (*Thunbergia alata*), some trailing petunia cultivars, million bells (*Calibrachoa* cultivars), lobelia and scaevola.

Deadhead perennials after flowering to keep them tidy. Sometimes, deadheading prompts a second flush of growth and a few more flowers. It's worth a try.

Shearing

If plants such as petunia, sweet alyssum and pansies have grown lank and leggy by midsummer, shear the plants back by one-half to two-thirds to trigger more compact stems and more flowers, then fertilize.

Sometimes plants grow lanky because they're not getting enough light or they're receiving too much nitrogen. In these cases, move them to a brighter spot or use a fertilizer higher in phosphorus.

Heat Stress

If plants wilt when the soil is still moist, heat and humidity might be the culprits. Giving them more water than they are able to use only adds to their stress. Instead, move the containers into the shade or out of hot wind, if practical. When it is time to water, do so in the morning, after plants have had a chance to recuperate during the lower nighttime temperatures. Wait until the heat spell passes before fertilizing. If your potted garden struggles every year when the temperature rises, choose larger containers made of better-insulating material, such as terra cotta or wood.

Naturally, plants that don't mind scorching temperatures, such as portulaca, cosmos, marigolds and verbena, fare better during hot days than those that like it cool—sweetpeas, impatiens, astilbe and butterfly flower (*Schizanthus pinnatus*), for example. Unfortunately, when we choose plants for our containers in the spring, we don't know what the summer will bring—cool and wet or hot and dry? If we could predict the weather, gardening would be so much easier, but not nearly as exciting.

Compacted Soil

Even loose, quick-draining potting mixes compact over time due to the frequent watering that containers require. Plants growing in the same pot from year to year will need repotting, usually every year or so. When water begins to pool on the surface instead of percolating down into the soil, it's time to repot.

Discolored Soil

A greenish cast on the surface of the soil indicates poorly drained soil and high acidity. Consider repotting in fresh soil, or lightly scratch the surface to allow more air to circulate.

A whitish cast on the soil surface is a sign of fertilizer salt build-up. Dry, brittle leaf edges also indicate too much fertilizer. Lightly scratch the surface of the soil and flush the container with water a few times to leach out the excess salts.

 # Overwintering Plants

If you live where winters are long and cold, you may want to save some of your favorite container plants for next year's garden. Called "overwintering," the term means carrying over plants until next spring, either by growing them indoors, storing them in a dormant state indoors or leaving them outside in a sheltered location.

Annuals aren't usually overwintered. Their natural lifespan is brief, and they're exhausted after producing the bountiful flowers and fruits you coaxed out of them over the summer. In this stressed state, they're susceptible to all kinds of maladies—whiteflies, aphids and spider mites. However, some tender perennials, hardy perennials, woody plants and tender summer bulbs are worth protecting and preserving. The method you use depends on the type of plant, its size, your available space and how ambitious you are.

Be realistic when it comes to choosing which plants to overwinter. Your windowsills will overflow if you don't exercise restraint. And if you have

Pests and Pestilence

Plants stressed from lack of water or nutrients are more susceptible to diseases and pests than are healthy specimens. Usually, the most troublesome pests are aphids, slugs and earwigs, and the most common fungus is powdery mildew.

Aphids

These tiny green, black or brown pests cluster on buds, shoots and the underside of leaves. They suck plant juices and produce a sticky honeydew substance that fosters the growth of molds and attracts ants. (Incidentally, ants aren't a plant problem—they merely indicate the arrival of aphids.) Remove infested stems or dislodge the aphids with a strong spray of water from the hose or spray with insecticidal soap. Insecticidal soap works only when it comes in contact with a pest, which means a few applications to all sides of flowers, leaves and stems over a week or two may be required. Ladybugs are natural predators.

Slugs

If you notice tiny, shiny trails of slime and chewed leaves, slugs are to blame. The soft-bodied mollusks are most active at night and when it's damp. Handpick them or use barriers such as strips of copper, pieces of screen or crushed eggshells to keep them from crawling into containers (they won't creep across rough surfaces). Ground beetles are natural predators.

Earwigs

Dark brown, pincer-tailed earwigs are wily creatures that devour decayed plant material and munch on leaves and petals. They do little significant damage, even when present in large numbers, but they can definitely mar a plant's appearance. Your best defense is to trap and destroy them. Earwigs congregate in dark, damp spots: place short lengths of garden hose, small pots stuffed with straw or shredded newspaper, or sections of folded or rolled newspaper near areas where they congregate. Empty or dispose of the traps each morning.

Powdery Mildew

Leaves, stems, flowers and buds with white or grayish patches are suffering from powdery mildew, caused by one of several hundred different fungi that are plant-specific. (Meaning the powdery mildew on verbena won't infect roses, and the mildew on roses won't infect zinnias.) It thrives in shady, damp sites where plants are crowded and air circulation is poor, often the case in containers packed with plants. Choose mildew-resistant varieties, if possible. If you can't live without zinnias, verbena and other mildew-prone plants, don't crowd them, try to keep water off the leaves and clip off infected leaves and stems. If the entire plant is seriously infected, get rid of it.

dozens of pots filled with dormant shrubs, roses and perennials in the garage, you may need to park in the driveway. Weigh the time and effort required to maintain a plant over winter against the cost of replacing it next season. Even experienced gardeners lose some plants. Sometimes the most practical solution is the compost pile.

Tender Perennials

In their native habitat, geraniums (*Pelargonium* spp. and cvs.), mandevilla, rosemary, flowering maple (*Abutilon* cultivars) and other tender perennials grow year-round. However, in areas where winters are well below freezing for months on end, these plants need to be brought indoors in order to survive. There are two methods for overwintering tender perennials indoors: bring in the entire plant in its container and treat it as a houseplant, or take cuttings and grow these as small plants (they'll be sturdy enough to plant outdoors next year).

Overwintering Plants Indoors

For this method stop fertilizing in late summer. A week or two before nights begin to turn cool, begin bringing the plants indoors at night to gradually acclimatize them to the lower light conditions and humidity levels. It's important to start this reverse hardening off process before plants get accustomed to cool fall nights; otherwise, they struggle with a change in temperature, as well as different light and humidity levels. If desired, treat plants with insecticidal soap to discourage pests from hitchhiking indoors. Cut back large plants, such as geraniums or coleus, by two-thirds to make them more manageable. Grow the plants in a cool room, if possible, where they will receive plenty of sunlight. Water when the soil begins to dry out, and don't start fertilizing until late winter.

Overwintering Cuttings

Some tender herbaceous perennials, such as geraniums, fuchsias, licorice plant (*Helichrysum petiolare* and cultivars) and coleus, grow well from cuttings, which take up less room indoors than mature plants. This method is also a good way to acquire more plants. Take four- or five-inch (10- or 12-cm) cuttings in late summer. Non-flowering stems are best, but if this isn't possible, pinch off flowers and flower buds. Snip off the bottom leaves, close to the stem, leaving two or three leaves at the top. Fill small pots with moist perlite, a combination of perlite and coarse sand, or soilless mix. Recut the bottom of the cutting at an angle, just below a leaf node. (The nodes where the bottom leaves were removed are where new roots will grow.) To speed up the root-making process, you may want to moisten the bottom of the cutting and dip it in a rooting hormone powder.

Using a pencil or skewer, make a hole in the soil no deeper than half the length of the cutting and insert it in the soil. (Making this hole prior to inserting the cutting is especially important if you use a rooting hormone, to prevent brushing off the powder.) Press soil around the base of the cutting. Loosely cover the cuttings with a clear plastic bag. Use toothpicks or bamboo skewers to keep the plastic off the leaves, or place the pot inside a large plastic bag and loosely fold the opening over the top of the plant. Place the cutting in a shady spot outdoors, or bring it indoors to root in bright, but not direct, sunlight. Keep the soil moist, but not soggy. In a few weeks, new leaves will form at the tip, indicating that roots have grown. Remove the plastic bag and place the plants indoors in a bright sunny window over winter, transplanting them to larger pots as needed.

Tender Bulbs, Corms, Rhizomes and Tubers

Remove the bulbs, corms, rhizomes or tubers of summer-blooming plants like canna lilies, dahlias, tuberous begonias and the like from containers after the plants die back in fall, and brush off soil. Let the bulbs dry outdoors for a few days, then store them in a cool, dark location in paper bags or cardboard boxes (not plastic) filled with barely damp sawdust, peat moss, vermiculite or perlite. Periodically check the moisture of the storage material. If it's bone-dry, moisten it slightly. You don't want the bulbs to shrivel up over winter. If they're too moist, though, they may rot or attract fungus.

If digging up bulbs seems like too much trouble, leave them in their containers, stop watering them when their leaves begin to die back in late fall and move them into a cool basement or next to the warmest wall of a garage. Most will resume growth the next spring—start watering and fertilizing when you see new green tips sprouting from the soil.

Lily bulbs never go completely dormant. If possible, sink the container in the garden and mulch heavily over winter, or store the bulbs in their container in a sheltered spot, similar to the method above.

Hardy spring-blooming bulbs that were forced (brought into early bloom) in pots and used in container displays can be planted in the garden after flowering is finished, but before foliage dies back. Most will bloom again in a couple of years. Forcing is an exhausting process for bulbs, and sometimes they fail to bloom again.

Hardy Perennials and Woody Plants

Overwintering container-grown hardy plants such as hard perennials, trees and shrubs requires different strategies.

Do Nothing

If the plants are in a large, frost-proof container, you can take your chances and do nothing. This works best if the plants are two zones hardier than the zone where you live. The soil temperature in pots above ground is lower than in the open ground, and alternate freeze/thaw conditions, especially if the container is located in full sun, can be damaging. Raise terra-cotta pots slightly off from the ground to reduce the risk of frost damage.

Move Containers

A more dependable method is to give the plants a thorough watering in the late fall, then move them, still in their containers, to a sheltered location, such as an unheated garden shed or garage. This keeps the plants a few degrees warmer than they would be if left above ground outdoors and also helps maintain fairly constant temperatures. Light isn't necessary because the plants are dormant, but they need moisture to keep them from desiccating. Some people loosely cover stored plants with a garbage bag—but don't close the bags tightly, or the plants may rot. Check the pots every two or three weeks to make sure the soil hasn't dried out completely.

Insulate Non-Moveable Containers

Rooftop and balcony gardeners sometimes have a small tree or large planter of perennials they want to maintain from year to year. Make sure planters can withstand the rigors of frost (wood is best) and insulate the interior surfaces before planting with two-inch (5-cm) thick panels of dense Styrofoam, cut to fit snuggly, but still allowing excess water to drain. Apply a mulch once the ground is frozen, and water just to keep the rootballs moist. (For more information on balcony gardening, see Chapter 10, "Gardening on High.")

Transplant

This method is more labor intensive. Remove the plant from the container, transplant it in the garden and mulch heavily. Next spring, either enjoy it in its new location or dig it up and move it back to the container.

glossary

Annual A plant that completes its life cycle in one season—it germinates, grows, flowers, sets seed and dies.

Bonemeal Organic fertilizer made from ground, steamed bones left over from meat processing; contains 12 percent phosphorus.

Bulb A storage organ made up of fleshy scales (modified leaves) that store food for a plant. Tulips and lilies grow from bulbs.

Chime rim The wide, flat rim found on standard, mass-produced terra-cotta pots. When manufacturers began using molds to mass produce terra cotta pots in the mid 1800s, the flat rim allowed the pots to be stacked in the kiln during firing, thereby saving space.

Clay The finest of the three particles found in soil, which is a mixture of clay, sand and silt.

Color echo Repeating a color to create unity or harmony in a garden setting, The term was coined in 1987 by Pamela Harper, a U.S. garden writer.

Color wheel The three primary and three secondary colors, usually shown in a circle, always appear in the following order: red, orange, yellow, green, blue and violet. Primary colors are red, yellow and blue. Secondary colors are orange, green and violet (combinations of the primary colors). Complementary colors lie opposite each other on the color wheel. Contrasting colors share no common pigment, such as red and yellow, yellow and blue, blue and red.

Composition (reconstituted) stone A mix of concrete and crushed stone that resembles real stone. It can be cast into various shapes.

Compost Decomposed plant materials used to improve garden soil.

Corm A swollen underground stem that stores food, much like a bulb, but without scales. Crocus grow from corms.

Cultivar A hybridized or selected plant. The word is a contraction of the term *culti*vated *vari*ety. For example, *Campanula persicifolia* 'Alba' is a cultivar of the species *Campanula persicifolia*. Abbreviations: cv. and cvs.

Deadheading Removing spent blooms to prolong flowering and to keep plants well groomed.

Dolomitic limestone Limestone mixed with magnesium.

Earthenware Coarse, porous fired clay, often glazed to make it less porous.

Focal point The center of interest in a design.

Forcing (bulbs) Inducing plants—in this case spring-flowering bulbs—to grow and flower by manipulating their environment.

Garden soil, garden loam A mixture of rock particles (clay, sand and silt), organic matter and other organisms. Soil with a balance of clay, sand and silt is called "loam," and is coveted by gardeners.

Gypsum Powdered pellets containing calcium sulfate; improves aeration in soil.

Half-hardy annual A plant that tolerates a light frost or two, and grows well during the cool weather of spring and fall, often less so in the heat of midsummer.

Hardening off Acclimatizing plants to a new environment, i.e., helping plants adjust from life in a greenhouse to life in the garden.

Hardiness zones Numerical ratings that denote plants' abilities to survive in various climates. The Canadian Plant Hardiness Zone Map and the USDA Plant Hardiness Zone Map were derived using different criteria, but both use winter hardiness as one indicator of a plant's hardiness.

Hardy perennial A perennial plant that withstands the climate of a given area.

Hayrack A long wire basket with one flat side that hangs off a wall or fence. The origin of the term is likely the racks used to hold feed for farm animals. Sometimes called "mangers."

Herbaceous perennial A non-woody plant that dies back (top growth dies and goes dormant) at the end of the growing season. The plant's roots survive winter and put forth new growth in the spring.

Humus Created by fungi and bacteria in soil.

K Symbol for potassium.

Leaf node The point on a stem where one or more leaves grow.

Limestone White powder or pellets made from limestone. When mixed with magnesium, it's called "dolomitic limestone." Used to neutralize or raise the pH (alkalinity) of soil.

Liner A lining in a container. A liner can serve three purposes: protect the outer container from water damage, provide space for excess water to drain in decorative pots with no drainage holes or reduce the rate of evaporation in small, porous pots.

Liquid transplant solution Concentrated liquid fertilizer high in phosphorus. Also contains indolebutyric acid, a synthetic root stimulator.

Long Tom Tall, narrow terra-cotta pots used for plants with deep roots; the term was coined by British potters in the mid-1800s.

Manger See hayrack.

N Symbol for nitrogen.

P Symbol for phosphorus.

Peat moss See sphagnum peat moss.

Perennial A plant that lives for more than two years.

Perennial grown as annual A perennial, usually native to tropical climates, considered an annual in northern climates because that's the way it behaves. In cold climates, it's grown for one season and then discarded when frost kills it. Often labeled as an annual, but technically this is incorrect.

Perlite Small, lightweight, white pellets that look like Styrofoam. Formed from ground volcanic rock heated until it expands to about 20 times its original size. Improves drainage and helps retain water.

Pot feet Usually manufactured pieces that raise a large pot a few inches above the surface it sits on. Sold in sets of three, pot feet are usually cast iron, terra cotta, concrete or plastic, and are decorative as well as practical.

Pot saucer Sits below a pot to collect excess water that drains from the bottom of a pot.

Potting soil Packaged soil that often contains sphaghum peat moss, sand and vermiculite or perlite.

Powdery mildew A plant disease caused by fungi that results in a white, powdery coating on stems, leaves and flowers.

Rhizome An underground stem that grows horizontally, usually near the surface. Cannas grow from rhizomes.

Rooting hormone powder Plant growth regulators applied to the end of cuttings to induce the formation of roots. The active ingredient is usually indolebutyric acid; may also contain a fungicide.

Sand The largest of the three major rock particles found in soil (the other two being silt and clay). Coarse or sharp sand is composed of larger pieces than beach, sandbox or horticultural sand.

Seed pans Short, squat terra-cotta pots used for germinating seeds.

Seed-starting mix See soilless mix.

Self-watering containers Containers with an inner pot for the plant and soil and an outer pot or reservoir that holds water in reserve. A wick bridges the two parts and pulls water up to the rootball as required.

Silt One of the three major rock particles in soil; larger than clay particles and smaller than sand.

Soil-based mix A growing medium for potted plants that contains soil.

Soilless mix A growing medium for potted plants that contains no soil.

Species A group of plants with similar characteristics in a genus. For example, *Campanula persicifolia* is a species in the *Campanula* genus. Abbreviations: sp. and spp.

Sphagnum moss The live moss that grows on top of a peat bog. Sphagnum moss plants absorb up to 20 times their weight in water and clump together. Often used for lining hanging baskets.

Sphagnum peat moss Derived from partially decomposed sphagnum moss and other plants in ancient bogs. It contains no nutrients, but holds five to 15 times its weight in water.

Staking Tying plants to poles or other supports to keep them upright.

Standard A plant trained to a single, bare stem with leaves and flowers at the top. Sometimes the top is clipped into a sphere or other fanciful shape.

Strawberry jar A tall pot with evenly spaced openings, called "pockets," spaced along the sides, usually made from terra cotta or glazed earthenware.

Superphosphate Fertilizer containing 20 percent phosphorus; made from rock phosphate treated with sulfuric and/or phosphoric acid.

Tender perennial A perennial that won't survive below-freezing temperatures.

Thumbs and thimbles Tiny terra-cotta pots used for seedlings.

Tilth Soil with a good structure is said to be "in good tilth"; also called friable soil.

Topsoil The top few inches (about 7 cm) of soil in a garden.

Tuber An underground stem with buds or eyes, which are the points from which the plant's above-ground stem grows.

Vermiculite Grayish-brown flakes or chips of mica treated with heat and pressure until they expand to many times their original size. Vermiculite aids water and fertilizer retention, and increases porosity in soilless and soil-based mixes.

Versailles boxes Wooden boxes created in the 17th century to house citrus trees and palms at Versailles in France. Now refers to any large, formal square plant container. Usually made from wood and painted white or dark green.

Water-retaining crystals, polymers or gels Translucent granules that absorb many times their own weight of water and release it when the soil surrounding them begins to dry out.

Water wand A lightweight metal or rigid plastic tube that connects to a garden hose at one end and has a spray head at the other. A pistol grip or shut-off valve near the hose end regulates the flow of water.

Woody or shrubby perennial Plants with stems and branches that persist above ground throughout the year. Roses and rosemary are shrubby perennials.

index

heat stress, 128–129

heavy-gauge steel wire containers, 14

Hedera helix, 38, 41, 47, 73, 95, 113

hedges, 124

Helichrysum petiolare, 39, 46, 47, 97, 131

heliotropes, 47, 76, 78

Heliotropium arborescens, 76

Hemerocallis cvs., 39, 73

hens and chicks, 5, 39, 94, 96

herb gardens, 104–105

herbaceous perennial, 136

herbal standards, 105

Heuchera spp. and cvs., 46, 47, 93–94

hibiscus, 67

high-rise gardens

    design, 122–124

    permanent plantings, 124

    plant choices, 121–122

    practical considerations, 120–121

    short-term plantings, 121

    survival strategies, 126

    weight of containers, 120–121

Hippophae rhamnoides, 122

hollies, 116

homemade mixes, 23–24

'Homestead' trailing verbena, 47

hoses, 32

Hosta plantaginea, 96

Hosta sieboldiana 'Elegans', 96

Hosta venusta 'Variegata', 96

hostas, 46, 82, 96

hummingbirds, 109

humus, 136

hyacinths, 108, 113

hydrangea flowerheads, dried, 116

I

Iberis umbellata, 40

Ilex verticillata, 116

impatiens, 38, 46, 76–77, 128, 129

Impatiens wallerana, 77

Impruneta (Italy), 10–11

indole-butyric acid, 36

informal design, 40, 124

Ipomoea batatus, 64, 91

Ipomoea batatus 'Blackie', 71, 74

Ipomoea batatus 'Marguerita', 46

Ipomoea tricolor, 89, 98

ivy geraniums, 75

J

Japanese anemones, 115

Japanese kerria, 116

Japanese maple, 124

Japanese painted ferns, 95

John Innes Composts, 25

'June' hosta, 46

K

K. *See* potassium

Kerria japonica, 116

Kingfisher daisies, 42, 47, 77

L

Labrador violets, 46

lady's eardrops. *See* fuchsias

lamiums, 97

Lantana camara, 67, 88

large containers

    benefits, 9

    location for, 4

    plant combinations and choices, 46

    soil mixes for, 23

    water gardens, 105–106

Lathyrus odoratus, 91, 98

Laurus nobilis, 67

lavender, 47

leached out nutrients, 34

lead containers, 14

lead look, 16

leaf lettuces, 106

leaf node, 136

lemon thyme, 47

licorice plants, 39, 46, 47, 97, 131

lilies, 47, 65, 73, 132

lily-of-the-nile, 66

lilyturf, 46

'Lime Green' nicotiana, 46

lime or limestone, 24, 136

'Limelight' licorice plant, 47

liners, 8, 136

liquid transplant solution, 136

loam, 20, 25, 136

loam-based compost, 25

lobelia, 46, 47, 102, 128

Lobelia erinus, 88

Lobelia ricardii, 88

Lobularia maritima, 83, 98

location, 3–4, 6, 50–51

long Tom, 12, 136

Lotus berthelotti, 46, 98

lotus vine, 46, 98

Lysimachia nummularia 'Aurea', 94

M

maintenance

    autumn container garden, 115–116

    cast-concrete containers, 15

    cast-iron containers, 14

    compacted soil, 129

    deadheading, 61, 68, 128

    discolored soil, 129

    fall container garden, 115–116

    fertilizers. *See* fertilizers

    heat stress, 128–129

    reconstituted stone containers, 15

    shearing, 128

    spring container garden, 114

    summer container garden, 115

    terra-cotta containers, 11

    watering. *See* watering

    winter container garden, 117

perilla, 46, 99
Perilla frutescens crispa, 46, 99
perlite, 20, 25, 137
Persian shield, 99
pests, 130
petunias, 38, 46, 47, 69, 78, 80–81, 128
Phalaris arundinacea 'Picta', 66
Phaseolus coccineus, 122
Philadelphus spp. and cvs., 122
Phormium tenax 'Atropurpurea', 114
phosphorus, 35, 136
photosynthesis, 35
Physalis alkekengi, 115
pinching off, 55
pineapple mint, 99
plant combinations and choices
    annuals, 45
    color, 42–44
    contrast textures and shapes, 41
    flower shapes and sizes, 42
    high-rise gardens, 121–122
    large planters, 46
    number of, 45–46
    perennials, 45
    practical considerations, 44
    scale, 41
plant labels, 57
plant types, 61–62
planting. *See* container planting
plastic containers, 15
Plectranthus madagascariensis, 78, 82, 99–100
Plectranthus madagascariensis 'Miller's Wife', 82
Polystichum arostichoides, 95
poor man's orchid, 70
portulacas, 39, 81, 98, 128, 129
Portulaca grandiflora. See portulacas
pot feet, 17, 137
pot marigolds, 70
pot saucers, 17, 137
potassium, 35, 136
potato vine, 90

potting compost, 25
potting soil, 21, 22, 25–26, 137
powdery mildew, 130, 137
practical considerations, 44
primroses, 113
Primula vulgaris cvs., 113
purple bell vine, 90–91
purple coneflower, 115

R
rain, 31, 33
'Rainbow' ajuga, 46
rainwater, 33
ranunculus, 113
Ranunculus asiaticus cvs., 113
reconstituted stone containers, 14–15, 135
red-twig dogwood, 116
regal geraniums, 75
removal from nursery pots, 53–54
repotting, 126
rhizomes, 62, 132, 137
Rhodochiton atrosanguineus, 90–91
Rhus typhina 'Dissecta', 121
ribbon grass, 66
Ricinus communis, 41
rooftop gardens, 123
    see also high-rise gardens
root stimulator, 36
rooting hormone powder, 137
rose gardens, 109–110
rosehips, 116
rosemary, 67, 100, 105, 130
roses, for standards, 67
Rosmarinus officinalis, 67, 100, 105, 130
Rudbeckia fulgida, 115
Russian olive, 122
rusted iron finish, 16

S
sage, 46, 82
Salix babylonica 'Tortuosa', 116
Salvia argentea, 91

Salvia coccinea, 82
Salvia farinacea, 39, 82
Salvia greggii, 73, 82
Salvia officinalis 'Purpurascens', 46, 82
Salvia splendens, 47, 82
salvias, 39, 46, 47, 73, 82, 91
sand, 26, 137
Sansevieria trifasciata, 41
saucers, 17, 137
Saxifraga spp., 108
scaevola, 85, 128
scale, 41
scarlet runner beans, 122
scarlet sage, 82
scented geraniums, 76, 105
Schizanthus pinnatus, 70, 129
sea buckthorn, 122
Seashell series impatiens, 77
sedges, 66
Sedum 'Autumn Joy', 115
Sedum sieboldii, 115
Sedum 'Vera Jameson', 115
sedums, 4, 46, 108, 115
seed pans, 12, 137
seed-starting mix, 21, 26, 137
self-watering containers, 32, 137
Sempervivum tectorum, 5, 39, 94, 96
Senecio cineraria, 46, 47, 69, 94
serviceberry, 121
shade combinations, 46
shearing, 128
shrubby perennials, 62, 138
shrubs, 124
Siberian peashrub, 121
silt, 137
silver sage, 91
site assessment, 3–4
sizes
    and container choice, 9
    and location, 4–5
    for vegetables, 103
slugs, 130
small containers